Metamorphosis

Kim Francisco

PRISTINE
PRESS AND MEDIA

ISBN
978-1-964804-82-8 (Paperback)
978-1-964804-81-1 (eBook)
978-1-964804-83-5 (Hardcover)

Dedicated to the memory of my loving wife, who for fifty years, stayed with me no matter if our home had indoor plumbing or not. She was the social spark plug of our relationship and my regular fishing buddy. The job often kept me away from home, which of course was when everything broke. She shrugged her shoulders and took care of it. After falling off a mountain the doctor told her I might never regain my senses and my best chance would be at home. She took me home, nursing me back to health. She is greatly loved and missed.

TABLE OF CONTENTS

Acknowledgments

Many people are always important in helping an author create a book. Many are named in the book. My apologies and thanks go to the people whose names I forgot or got wrong. My only excuse is old age.

Metamorphosis was my third book, but was the most difficult to publish. My wife's frontal temporal degeneration became much worse just as the manuscript was finished. Not having the time needed for self-publication, I chose to use one of many publishers' assistant companies that exist for authors today. I made the wrong choice. I won't name them, but acknowledge that they completed a first edit. On my second try, I found Lewis Publications. Brittany and her staff there have been excellent to work with, which is why you are reading this book now. Unfortunately, Lewis Publishing suffered many problems that prevented them from publishing within the agreed-upon time. Due to a royalties dispute, I republished and re-recorded my books with Pristine Press and Media.

PREFACE

Memoirs are an individual's memories; I've learned that other people's memories are often different from mine. The events in this book are from my notes, records, and memory. I've told and retold many of these stories over the years, which helped keep the memories alive. Some unintentional editing may have occurred in the retelling.

I recently shadowed a high school history teacher to complete the requirements to be a substitute teacher in Iowa. The decade they were studying was the 1960s—a shock to me. I knew they weren't current events, but it was ten years of my life; how could it be history? I understood it was history when the students asked about the controversy over the draft. The book had left out what the draft was or why it was controversial. The teacher was stumped; he was too young to know what the draft was, let alone what controversy it caused. I was able to clear things up. I felt both valuable and old.

This book is a decade later, beginning in the fall of 1973, when my last book ALIBI MIKE ended. Alaska and the Department of Fish and Game I describe has changed since then. Fisheries' biology has changed. As a lifetime member of the American Fisheries Society, I still receive their publications and try to stay current. I've also tried to keep up with Alaska through my friends there and am astounded at the pace and breadth of change.

Unlike many (most) memoirs, mine doesn't deal with overcoming dysfunctional families, illness, or other disasters. Instead, it's about someone who, thanks to being raised by a supportive, loving family, good luck, hard work, and a little intelligence, had a very successful life. Reading about the experiences of explorers and scientists caused me to crave adventure. Not sure where I found the courage, because I'm a total coward. I've never done anything without fear, but tried to live by the rule expressed by a poster in my dorm room: "Behold the turtle; never gets anywhere without sticking its neck out."

I hope you, my reader, are entertained. If you are inspired to try something you've dreamed of, great! Suppose you pick up a few techniques helpful in dealing with life successfully; wonderful. You surely will learn how not to accomplish some things.

CHAPTER ONE

❧❧❧❧❧

FLYING WITHOUT WINGS

What! Wow, I've never seen El Coyote's undercarriage without a lift. Where am I? Seem to be moving away, fast, and up. Whoa!

El Coyote, my 1962 Toyota Land Cruiser, performed a gymnastic move, flipping end for end while completing a full rotation. It planted the landing on all four tires, still pointing in the original direction of travel. It had finished crossing the bridge where the somersault began. As it stuck the landing, a terrible groan of overstressed steel and shock absorbers emanated from the car. It squatted, the differentials touching the ground. El Coyote stood up, but not straight since the front left tire had blown. Jim was sitting in the middle of the bridge where he had fallen when the passenger door sprung open. Dave was staggering out the driver's door. He had had a death grip on the steering wheel, the seatbelt holding him in place, experiencing the somersault from the inside.

My climb skyward slowed to a stop. *It's a long way down! The landing will hurt! Oh no! I'm turning over.* Landing feet first seemed preferable to headfirst. I flapped my arms and kicked my feet, trying to return my body to a feet-down position, to no avail. *Shit, my center of gravity must be above my waist.* As the ground began racing towards my face, individual pieces of gravel became visible. I wrapped my right arm across my eyes. The pain began as my elbow dug into the gravel. I was sure I was plowing a furrow through the gravel as my body slammed into the road.

Am I alive? Guess so, I seem to hear distant voices. What are they saying?
"Dead or hurt?"

"Let's turn him over."

"No!" I screamed.

"He said something. Did you hear it?"

"Just a moan or death rattle."

No! Try again. I tried to take a deep breath for volume. Pain stabbed through my chest. *Shit, all my ribs are broken. Got to stop them from moving me.* As I felt a hand on my shoulder, I painfully drew a small breath and forced out, "Don't touch me."

"He says not to touch him, I think."

"I took first aid once. They said not to move people unless they were in danger. I don't see any blood."

"At least he's alive. Wonder how long until someone comes?"

"His foot is moving!"

I had wiggled my toes in each boot. That worked and didn't hurt, so I tried pushing the right boot toe through the gravel when Jim or Dave noticed my foot move. I still couldn't recognize their voices, which seemed very far away. Both feet moved, so I gently tried bending my knees, one at a time. *That works and doesn't hurt. Didn't break my legs. Try lifting my legs. See how my hips are doing.* I whimpered as pain shot through my chest. *Won't try that again! How about hands?* I carefully pushed the fingers on my left hand where they lay against my hip. *That works. It doesn't seem to hurt the hip.* I slowly and carefully tested the left arm and finally brought it up by my head.

"Kim, your arm works. How are you?" a concerned Jim asked.

I tried to breathe to answer, but pain stabbed through my chest. I just growled.

"Don't think he wants any help yet," Dave said.

I continued a careful examination of my body and limbs. My right arm felt broken; I wasn't sure how many pieces the bones might be in. Legs seemed all right. The pain in my chest scared me the most. *Internal injuries? Is internal bleeding killing me? Hope just the wind knocked out of me. Wishful thinking, you're dying. What did the first aid course say to do for internal injuries? Don't move patient until medical professionals are available. A big help here.*

I lay quietly in the gravel, which didn't hurt much. I felt a hand on my shoulder. "Don't touch me." Inhaling after speaking hurt, but my voice was stronger, though still muffled by the gravel and my right arm.

Jim said, "Okay, I won't move you. Dave's checking out the car. Maybe we can get you to a hospital."

Fat chance. The nearest hospital is probably in Vancouver. How could they get me in? Roll me over onto my sleeping bag? Carry it like a stretcher?

"Looks like just a flat tire on the front driver-side. Think if we change tire we can keep going," I heard Dave say.

"Let's do it. I think Kim needs a doctor."

"Yeah, well, the spare's in the back, but I don't know where the jack is."

"Under the right back seat," I spoke into my arm.

"What?"

"Under the right back seat," I said louder into my arm.

"Under the right back seat?"

I nodded my head in the affirmative. *Nodding doesn't hurt; at least my neck isn't broken.*

I heard their footsteps in the gravel as they returned to El Coyote. I could hear them talking but couldn't make out the words. They were too far away. Then I heard steps approaching.

Jim said, "Kim, I brought your rain gear and jacket. Thought you be warmer if I covered you up."

"Thanks," I murmured into my arm. I felt Jim gently spread the jacket and rain gear over me. *Good idea. I am getting cold.* I heard him returning to help Dave unpack the back enough to get under the rear right seat. I lay in the cold, wet gravel, and started to shiver in spite of the coverings Jim had laid on me. *Great, they'll tell Mom I survived the accident with just a broken arm but died of hypothermia. Might be a sad enough story to get me my fifteen seconds of fame. Or is it fifteen minutes?*

"How do you release the spare tire?" I heard Dave holler.

Why does he want to release the spare tire? Does he mean he doesn't understand the three lug nuts? How can I answer with my mouth in my arm? Guess if I'm going to get rescued, I need to help.

Jim's voice, very close, suddenly interrupted my thoughts. "Kim, can you tell me how to release the tire?"

"Yeah, just take the hubcap off the spare and take the lug nuts off," I said, pulling my mouth away from my arm to be heard. *No pain. Good. Doesn't hurt as much to breathe.*

"Oh, but what about releasing the tire mount?"

Huh, that doesn't make sense. He must think the tire and mount have to come off. "No, no, you leave the tire mount alone. Just take the spare off."

"Okay, we'll try that," Jim said uncertainly as he walked away.

Crap, it isn't that hard. Guess they need help. I thought Dave had some mechanical experience. Knew Jim was pretty much helpless.

Obscenities drifted back to me from where Dave and Jim were struggling with the spare. I shivered with the cold, noticing that shivering didn't hurt, and I seemed to be breathing normally again.

Damn it, roll over onto left arm. I rolled slowly and gently over my left side onto my back. *So far so good. Right arm really hurts. I'm kind of tangled in my jacket and rain gear. See if they can hear me.* "Hey, just take the hubcap off the spare," I said in a normal tone of voice, not being able to breathe deeply enough to raise my voice. The obscene muttering continued uninterrupted. *Fuck, they can't hear me. Need to be louder. Here goes.* I took a big breath and said louder to the sky, "Just take the hubcap off." *Wow, didn't hurt. Maybe I just had the wind knocked out of me?*

"Kim said something. He's rolled over!" I heard footsteps coming through the gravel towards me as Jim and Dave came up on either side of me. "How the hell did you do that?" one of them asked.

"Carefully," I snapped. "Help me sit up but stop if I tell you to."

They knelt next to me, each one pushing a hand through the gravel under each of my shoulders. "Ready?"

"Let's do it." With a grimace in anticipation of the pain I tightened my muscles in my abdomen and dug in my heels so my leg muscles could assist. Jim and Dave carefully and slowly lifted a shoulder, raising me to a sitting position. There was very little pain except my arm, which really throbbed with pain. *That wasn't so bad. Maybe I'm going to live after all.* "Guess I just had the wind knocked out of me, except for my right arm. I think it's broken."

"It sure is bloody. Do you need a bandage? Jim asked.

Looking at my arm, I said, "No it seems to be clotting up alright. No bones sticking out. I'm just cold."

"Better get your jacket on," Jim said.

"Yeah, help me stand, and it will be easier."

Dave said, "Jim, take his left shoulder. I'll just lift him by his belt on this side."

"Just keep your hands out of my pockets," I said.

"He's gonna live, cracking wise again already," Dave added.

"On three," Jim said as he began counting. On three, Dave lifted me by the seat of my pants, Jim raised my shoulder, and I pulled my legs in under me and rose to my feet. Jim got the jacket onto my left arm. As we reached the right, I found it too painful to move it away from where it rested at the bottom of my ribs. I was too cold to wait for them to fashion a sling so Dave just pulled the jacket over my shoulder and right arm. It was tight, but they managed to zip the jacket up which provided some support for my injured arm. Ready to face the world again, I walked back to El Coyote with them.

I walked around, inspecting for damage. The left front tire was blown. Dave explained, "I was trying to keep the car on the two planks." These were set at the width of the logging trucks, too wide for El Coyote's wheelbase.

"Geez, I told you when you started driving that the planks were spaced for the logging trucks, and you couldn't keep the L.C. on both. Just pick one side or the other and go slow."

"Yeah, but I was sure I could do it," Dave replied.

"Great, you trapped the tire's sidewall against the edge of the plank and blew the tire. That's what tipped the car over on its right side." I looked at the bridge, L.C. and tried to remember what I'd seen looking down. "It must have slid across the bridge on its side until it hit the road on the other side. See how the road is higher than the bridge? Somehow hitting that flipped it end for end, and rolled it side to side. I saw Jim on the bridge and the open door while I was flying through the air."

"I fell against the door and out when she started to roll. It just left me on the bridge," Jim added.

"It was quite a sight from up above," I interjected.

"You think that was something to see? You should have been on the inside holding on to the steering wheel. What a fucking ride," Dave concluded.

Following my directions—I was no help physically—we got the spare off, the car jacked-up, the flat tire off and the spare on. We hung the flat tire on the spare tire mount, reloaded the car and were ready to go. Dave turned the key. The engine cranked but wouldn't start. After several long tries I said, "Hold it, we don't want to run the battery down. Let's look under the hood."

"You know what to do?" Jim said.

"No, I don't know what's wrong until I look. I hope there's just a disconnected wire or something," I replied.

Dave said, "It's all a mystery to me. Hell, that was the first time I changed a tire."

"Really? My father even made my sister change a tire before letting her drive. She really hated it. Had to stand on a lug wrench to get the nuts off. Quite the show. Thought Dad was going to have a stroke. He wasn't a calm teacher." I was looking around under the hood Dave had lifted for me poking around with my left hand. Jim didn't seem interested in being "hands on" under the hood so I explained to Dave how to check that plug wires were tight both at plug and distributor. The battery connections were tight, even the ground to the frame. "Probably not battery connections or it wouldn't turn over, but working on engines is kind of magical. Sometimes they just want a little love and attention, then for no reason everything seems to work."

Jim commented, "Is that why you're always telling us to think positive about the car and not say anything bad about it?"

"Yep, guess I'm really superstitious and not scientific. Everything seems okay. Dave, go ahead and try to start it again. I'll watch." Dave turned the key, and I watched all the pulleys and belts go through their motions. "Stop, come on out." Dave met me at the left side of the engine. "See the wing nut there on top of the air filter?" I said pointing with my left hand.

"Yeah, you want me to take it off?"

"Yep, the cover too. I'll be able to see how the butterfly valve is working. And if the carb is getting gas."

Dave went to work disassembling the air filter, while I pondered how I would get high enough to see into the top of the carburetor with one hand. As he pulled the air filter out of the canister, I went around to the front and started to climb up on El Coyote's huge front steel bumper, more of a battering ram than bumper. I tried and failed on my first attempt. I didn't realize how important using my right hand to pull myself up was to be climbing. I switched my leading leg and reached in to grab a pulley and pulled myself up onto the bumper.

Standing on the bumper, I could lean over the air filter canister and see into the mouth of the carb with my left arm supporting me by resting my left hand on the valve cover. "Okay, Dave, try starting it again."

Concerned, Jim said, "Kim you'll get caught in the engine!"

"Nah, I'm safe, done this a million times. Just never left-handed. Turn it over," I shouted. Dave cranked the engine and I saw gas squirt into the carb. "Stop. See the knob on the dash that says choke?"

"Yeah," Dave replied.

"Pull it all the way out. Then try again."

I saw the choke close, the butterfly and the car turned over and over. "Stop."

I climbed down and got back into the car. Jim followed me in. "I'm hoping it's flooded and if we give it some time it will start. Otherwise, we're screwed."

A half hour passed slowly. Jim and I entertained Dave with the story of the previous spring when Hildebrand, Jim, and I had taken Hildebrand's Maverick to Circle, as far north as the Alaska highway system would take you. (That's changed now that the Trans-Alaska pipeline haul road was taken over by Alaska's DOT.)

"Circle is the end of the road and located on the Yukon River. One of the 'requirements' to graduate from cheechako to a sourdough is to pee in the Yukon River. Which neither Jim nor Don had done, so we made a road trip."

"Shit, guess I need to do that too," Dave interjected.

"Remind me when we get back and we can take you on a pee raid," I continued. "The trip to Circle was uneventful. We had to take a small hike to get to a spot private enough for the guys to whip them out and take the mandatory pee. As we walked back to El Coyote a cold spring rain began. We didn't have rain gear. A lesson in Alaskan travel be ready for any kind of weather."

"Don drove us south through the rain. After crossing the high point in the pass through the White Mountains, the rain turned to snow up there," Jim added. "Then the gravel highway turned into a rutted mess."

"Spring runoff, thawing road, and heavy equipment travel." I assumed that's what caused that. I continued, "The road had small gullies across it. The Maverick bottomed out on everyone. As we bounced along, I was in the backseat, which always seems to bounce more than the front, and I heard a new rattle, then a bang from under my seat. I looked out the back window and saw the gas tank come bouncing out from under the car being towed by the rubber gas line. 'Stop!' I screamed. There was a vision of fire and explosion flashing through my mind."

"Why?" Don asked.

"Your gas tank fell off. You have to stop to put it back on!"

"How could the gas tank fall off?" he said without even slowing down.

"The ruts in the road knocked it off. 'Stop or we're going to die!' I shouted hopelessly. At which point the gas in the carburetor and fuel line was exhausted and the engine coughed and sputtered to a halt."

"I was never so glad to run out of gas," Jim added.

"The engine died!" Don said.

"Yeah, it's out of gas. Your gas tank fell off about half a mile ago," I said disgustedly.

"Oh."

"We piled out of the car. Don said, 'What do we do now?'

" 'We walk back and get the gas tank and any pieces of the mounting bracket we can find. I'll try and put everything back together with my multitool,' I told him, heading for the gas tank, which was only a hundred feet behind. Jim and Don followed along behind. At the gas tank, I sent everyone in different directions searching for any pieces that came off. All we found was the rubber gas hose."

"I found that," Jim said proudly.

"The good news was the hose clamps were still on each end of the hose. Back at the car I loosened the clamps and put one end of the hose back on the gas tank. Then laying down on my back in the wet, cold gravel, I tried unsuccessfully pushing myself under the Maverick. There just wasn't enough clearance for my fat body. We got out the jack and tried to jack up the rear of the car but the small base on the jack sunk into the wet gravel instead of raising the car. 'Shit, fuck, damn. Next time we bring my Land Cruiser. Look around and see if you can find a flat piece of wood or a rock we can put the jack on.'"

Jim said, "I found a big, flat rock that Kim said would work. It didn't."

"That's true, on the first try I placed the jack on top of the rock and tried to slide them under the car's jacking point. It was too high. Don had a flat piece of wood he had found. I used that like a shovel to scrape a hole for the rock and jack. Every scrape took out gravel and shortened the shovel. It was a near thing, but I had a deep enough hole for the rock and jack. I finished jacking the car up as high as it would go. The contraption looked unstable. 'Who wants to hold the jack while I crawl underneath?'"

"We didn't understand what he wanted," Jim said, "But I volunteered. Kim had me put my hands on each side of the jack. Tell me if it starts to tip over, push it back up straight. I told him. He didn't like that idea and I said, 'Don't worry if it falls the tires will keep it from crushing me.'"

"Fuck, that could kill you! Don't do it. We'll just wait for help," Don said.

Jim said, "That did it for me, anything to look macho. I held the jack."

"Yeah, and I crawled under, wondering if I had told Jim the truth or whether I would be killed by crushing or the exploding gas tank."

"You're both nuts. Jim isn't strong enough to hold a jack up," Dave said.

Jim said, "I am and I did."

I went on. "Looked like a simple job, just a matter of connections, the gas line lifting the gas tank up and strapping it back in place with the steel strap hanging there."

"As I hooked the loose end of the strap with my left hand holding the sloshing gas tank in place with my right, I discovered the missing safety bolt. The strap hooked over a lip on the frame, but to keep it from bouncing off, there was a hole in the hook to bolt to the frame. The bolt was gone. I crawled out swearing. The toolbox in my L.C., like most toolboxes, had a collection of nuts and bolts that had accumulated over the years. But all Don had was the tire changing kit. We needed a little bolt. I said, 'Let's walk back to that DOT maintenance camp and see if they'll give us a bolt.'"

" 'What camp?'" we said, as neither Don nor I had seen it. Which really annoyed Kim," Jim said.

"Well, we were on a trip so you guys could see Alaska outside the campus, and you hadn't even seen that maintenance camp!" I said.

Jim continued. "Don said, 'What about my car?'"

"You think a moose will steal it? Then I asked Kim if we might see a moose," Jim said.

" 'Not you fuckers, you can't even see a maintenance camp.' He was still pissed. But then he said, 'There's a chance if you walk quietly,'" Jim said.

"What about bears?" Don asked.

"I told him they're still hibernating, but you sure don't want to be the first piece of meat they see when they come out." I said, feeling mean.

Jim interrupted, "Kim likes to play on people's fears."

"Hey, that's good, clean fun," Dave defended me.

I continued with the story. "We walked. It took about forty-five minutes. The Steese was only maintained in the summer. It had just reopened and there didn't seem to be much going on. Maybe the summer crew hadn't returned yet. We heard someone working. We followed the sound. We found a man working on a large yellow Caterpillar bulldozer.

" 'Hi, I'm Kim Francisco.' I always give people my name, it seems to reassure them.

"He finished tightening whatever he was working on and looked at me. 'Hi, Joe Mechanic!' (I don't remember his name.) I put my hand out, he wiped his on a rag and took mine, saying as we shook, 'What d'ya need?'

" 'We're coming back from Circle and the gas tank fell off the car. Found the strap and got it put back on, but we need a safety bolt. Would you have a small nut and bolt or some safety wire?'

" 'Sure, follow me.' He led us over to a workbench, where on the wall was a cabinet filled with drawers, which were filled with an assortment of nuts and bolts. 'Help yourself.' He returned to his work with Don and Jim following him.

"I peeked into drawers until I hit ones that looked to be the right size. To play it safe, I took the one that looked right plus one larger and one smaller. I found lock nuts that fit. Then seeing the roll of safety wire on the bench, I thought I better use the old belt and suspenders approach, and clipped off a piece of wire, just in case. I returned to Joe who I think was getting a little annoyed by Jim and Don's questions."

"Hey, he was an interesting dude," Jim defended himself.

"Yeah, he was a nice guy. I told him what I'd taken and offered to bring back the ones we didn't use. Then I asked what we owed.

"Smiling, he said, 'Don't bother bringing them back and you don't owe me anything. You paid for them when you bought gas for the trip. I don't think Eagan (the Governor) will miss them.'

'Thanks," I said, shaking his hand again. We headed back to the car.

"I was trudging along, muttering to myself about how stupid I was not to have driven the L.C. instead of Don's wind-up toy. Jim and Don were still enjoying their great Alaskan adventure, leaving grumpy me behind. As we climbed a hill, I was startled to attention by their screams.

"Bear! Bear! Run for your life."

"Stupid, you never run from a bear," I shouted as they passed. They didn't slow down."

Jim said, "Yeah, we couldn't figure out what he was waiting for."
Dave asked, "Why not run?"

"That's the surest way to make it think you are food. I stayed put because bears are a lot faster than people, one of them would have already been snacking on Jim or Don. That's also why running isn't a good idea. I looked up the road through my rain-smeared glasses, to see what struck fear into our fearless pair. I could see a small, dark creature ambling slowly down the road. If it was a bear, it was a cub. Which, if its mama is around, is not good. Taking my glasses off for a clearer view, I still couldn't tell what I was looking at. I stood puzzled as it approached me. Then through the wind and my stocking cap I could hear the grumble of the unhappiest creature in the forest: a porcupine. Everyone I've encountered was grumbling like it had just lost the most precious thing in life. I turned and called to Jim and Don—they were waiting to watch me be torn from limb to limb, 'Hey, it's just a porky. Come back, I'll show you.'

"Their hesitant walk back resulted in the porky passing me. I walked alongside it towards the guys but out of reach of its tail."

"Won't it throw its quills at you?" one of them asked.

"Nah, old wives' tale. You have to touch them or get close enough for one to hit you with its tail," I told them.

" 'Why isn't it running away?'

" 'They're used to being ignored. If we started moving towards it, it would run for the nearest place to hide its head or roll up in a ball.' The porky, being a little concerned at the growing crowd, angled away from us towards the edge of the road but continued on its way.

" 'Why is it walking down the road?'

"I turned back towards the car. 'Because it's the easiest way. Unfortunately for porcupines, that's why you see so many of them run over. Doesn't seem to affect the population; guess sex isn't as hard as it looks.'

"My attempt at humor earned me a small groan. Upon reaching the car I once again crawled underneath. One of the bolts fit, mostly. It was a little loose in the hole. I figured the hole had become enlarged with wear which is why the tank fell off. The next size larger bolt was too big. I asked Don if Mavericks were made overseas and used metric. He didn't know. With the gas tank once again in place, Don tried to fire it up. I had to explain that he had to keep cranking because the gas pump needed to refill all the lines. The battery was weakening when it caught, and the little engine once again had us headed for Fairbanks. We made about half a mile."

"Aw, it was further than that," Jim added.

"With a clatter and bang the gas tank hit the gravel. Don was faster on the brakes this time, so it was still connected to the gas line when we surrounded it at the back of the car. After crawling underneath again, I discovered the 'snap' that attached the strap had broken.

"Crawling out, I said, 'The good news is the new bolt held. The bad news is it held so well the whole snap broke off. We are screwed.'

"'You can't fix it?'"

"'Mother Teresa couldn't fix it.'"

"'What do we do?'"

"'Open the trunk. That gas line is stretched from towing the tank down the road; maybe we can put the tank in the trunk.'"

"'How will we close the trunk?' Don asked as he opened it.

"'One problem at a time please.' Jim and I squatted down and picked up the gas tank and tried to put it in the trunk. We tried several positions but always ended with it teetering on the edge. The hose just wasn't long enough.

"As we stood in the rain, scratching our heads, a semitruck with a flatbed loaded with a Caterpillar dozer pulled up and stopped.

"A grizzled, old sourdough stepped out. His Carhartt overalls had seen better days. They were almost black with dirt and grease, and where his wool long johns showed through, they were torn and worn.

He looked like a man who could help. He took in the scene and greeted us with, 'Looks like ya got some trouble.'

"'Yes, sir. Managed to reattach the tank the first time but the clip broke off and the hose isn't long enough to put it in the trunk,' I said.

"'Hmmm.' He rubbed the stubble on his chin with his hand. 'Lock her up. Only room for two of you in the cab. One will have to ride on the Cat.'"

"I rode the Cat. It was fun at first," Jim said.

"Yeah, I felt guilty sitting in the cab with the heater, making me realize how chilled I was, like now. Supposed to share body heat to prevent hypothermia, but I'll need to get a lot worse before I'll cuddle with you guys.

"The driver dropped us at a service station in Fairbanks. Jim, who had started his ride on the Cat in an animated pantomime of driving, was a subdued, shaking, teeth chattering victim of early hypothermia. I called the dorm. Luckily Bill Benitez was in and picked us up."

"Pissing in the Yukon almost killed me," Jim said.

CHAPTER TWO

"YOU CAN AFFORD THIS, CAN'T YOU?"

We spent an hour or so jumping in and out of El Coyote as I thought of something to check to get the engine to start. Finally, the battery

was beginning to run down, and as it turned the engine over more slowly, I slumped behind the steering wheel, exhausted by my injuries and the efforts to restart the car.

"That's it. I'm out of ideas. Something serious broke. It needs a real mechanic," I said to the steering wheel, but Dave and Jim overheard me.

"Should we start walking?" Jim asked.

"It would be something to do until we can hitch a ride," Dave offered.

Leaning back in the seat I muttered, "Let me see the map?"

Jim handed me the road map of British Columbia we had picked up at our last gas stop. He handed it to me, asking, "Do you know where we are?" "No, but we have about half a tank of gas. We must have come about a hundred fifty miles since our last stop. Which should put us about here," I said, poking my finger on the map. "The next gas stop was going to be Stewart, we're more than halfway, but it's still a long walk. Like sixty miles long. You guys can do what you want, but I'm staying here out of the rain with the hood up. Someone will be more likely to stop for a broken-down car than three longhaired, bearded, bums."

"Hey, I resemble that remark," cracked Dave. We all laughed, but it sounded a little forced.

"Hey," Jim said, "I got a couple of red bandanas. You think they would make someone more likely to stop?"

"Good idea," Dave and I said in unison.

Jim dug into his pack and produced the bandanas. Then he and Dave got out of the L.C. and tied one to the front of the hood, which when raised, rested on the windshield projecting above it. The second one was tied to the top of the radio antenna.

I closed my eyes while they worked and don't remember if I heard them return to the car, but I fell asleep. I don't know for how long, but I was awakened by excited voices saying, "He stopped!"

I opened my eyes to see through the rain-streaked windshield a flatbed semi backing up towards us. Jim and Dave were out of the car, explaining our predicament to a large, middle-aged man in a wool shirt and brown duck work pants that were well-streaked with oil and grease where he had wiped his hands. As I joined them, he was already climbing up on the flatbed. He said, "I'll release the winch and hand you guys the hook. Take it back and hook it to your frame, and I'll tow you up onto the truck. I have a couple of ramps in the back. One of you can help me set them to your wheelbase."

With the driver in charge, I huddled, nursing my arm, watching. I only stuck my oar in when Jim started to put the winch hook on the Land Cruiser front bumper.

"No, Jim, loop the cable through those two hooks behind the bumper, then put the hook on the cable," I instructed.

"Oh, I see. Kind of lasso the hooks. That looks better."

The trucker finished positioning the ramp he was working on. He stepped onto the cable and gave it a strong tug, which tightened the loop on the L.C.'s tow hooks. "Nice hooks. Did you add those?"

"No, standard equipment," I answered.

He stepped over the cable, checked Dave's ramp, walking up it onto the back of the flatbed. "Okay, one of you needs to drive, you other two stand clear in case the cable lets go."

Dave was closest to El Coyote's left door, so he climbed into the driver's seat. The trucker walked up the flatbed to the winch. I moved to the left side even with the rear of the L.C.

Remember Dad's story about the sailor on the tugboat, who got cut in half when the cable snapped and whipped across the deck. Hope Dave does better driving up the ramps than he did crossing the bridge.

The winch began making a grinding noise as the cable tightened and El Coyote slowly moved to the ramps, then up onto the flatbed. The trucker winched it up tight behind the cab of the semi. "Dave, put it in first and put on the parking brake," I called.

"Yeah, give me a hand putting these chains through these," the trucker said, touching the L.C.'s rear "bumpers": horseshoe-shaped flat steel welded into the frame. The chains were then hooked to eyes on the edge of the flat bed. The trucker put chain tighteners on each and tightened them down. El Coyote wasn't going to move during its ride.

Jim volunteered to reprise his "role" as driver by staying in the L.C., but the trucker said there was room in the cab for everyone. Not sure if I dozed off or miles of a mountain road with impressive vistas at every turn just became so routine, I don't remember anything until we stopped at the only service station in Stewart, B.C.

We thanked our trucker repeatedly. He refused the one-hundred dollars I offered, saying "You just help anyone you find stranded next to the road." Then while I signed the work order authorizing the station to diagnose El Coyote's problem and give me a repair estimate, Dave and Jim pushed El Coyote to an empty parking place next to the garage. Our next question was "Where can we camp?" The local campground was closed for the winter, but they pointed out an empty forested lot across the street and said they didn't think anyone would mind if we camped there, as long as we used the station's restroom and didn't leave trash around. Then Jim asked, "Where can Kim get his arm checked out?"

"At the hospital. It's on the other side of town." The attendant replied.

Do I need an emergency room? This arm does still really hurt. But first aid is okay. I don't want to walk across town.

Looking up from the paperwork, I said, "I'm okay. Don't need a hospital."

Dave and Jim insisted. The attendant called a teenager in overalls out of the garage. "Take this guy over to the hospital in the wrecker." That ended the discussion.

Dave and Jim said, "You go. We'll take the gear across the street and set up camp. If the nurse is cute, ask if she has two friends."

Resigned to my fate, I said, "Okay," and followed the teenager to the wrecker. I opened the door with my still good left arm. *Should have thought to protect my face with left arm. Wonder if credit card and travel check people will recognize my signature. First time I've used that credit card Mom gave me for emergencies. Guess after two years she won't mind once. Probably can pay for repair with travelers' checks. Just use credit card as security.*

"Here we are."

"Thanks for the ride," I said, getting out. The hospital was two stories, which I think made it the tallest building in town, government issue square box. The white paint needed to be redone. The wooden shiplap siding was beginning to show through. I walked inside and the place seemed deserted. Nothing happening and not a soul insight. I walked up to the reception counter and said "Hello". Nothing happened. There was a bell on the counter with a sign "Ring for service." *Hate ringing bells. Seems rude somehow. Wonder where I got that idea.*

After waiting for a while in hopes someone would notice me, I finally gently rang the bell. After a moment, a twenty-something woman in a tight, white uniform, stepped out into the reception area.

"Hi. Can I help you?" she asked brightly. Which seemed inappropriate considering how I felt, between pain, a broken car, and my wet, cold condition.

"Yes, I was thrown from a car during an accident. My right arm has some serious road rash and I think it might be broken." *And here comes more paperwork to fill out lefthanded.*

"Oh dear," she said, taking in my appearance and demeanor. "We'll get you checked out and cared for." She pressed a buzzer. An older gray-haired woman also in hospital whites appeared at my left arm. Same uniform except she had a little white hat, more of a tiara or crown since there was no top. *Hat some symbol of rank?* "This young man was thrown from a car in an accident. His right arm is injured and may be broken," the receptionist said to her. To me she said, "This is nurse Hathaway. She'll see you get the care you need. What's your name?"

"Richard Kim Francisco, but please call me Kim."

"Mr. Francisco, do you need a wheelchair, or can you walk?" the nurse asked.

Do you see a wheelchair? How do you think I got in here? "I can walk."

"Follow me please." And the nurse headed down the otherwise deserted hallway. We passed several closed doors marked only with numbers. We arrived at an identical door, except for the number, and she led me in. There was a machine, that as I studied it, I recognized it from old movies as an X-ray machine. *Wonder when the mad scientist will appear.*

"Please take off your jacket and shirt," interrupted my thoughts of old horror movies. With some difficulty, I struggled out of my jacket and shirt with just my clumsy left arm and teeth for help. *Wonder when the nurse will give me a hand instead of messing with the machine.* As I struggled with my shirt, she finally seemed satisfied with her adjustments to the X-ray and turned to look at me with my teeth clamped into my left cuff as I tried to pull my hand through. I was unable to unbutton the cuff with my injured right hand, and a normally simple task was very hard.

"Let me help."

"Thank you." *At last.*

She quickly unbuttoned the cuff and pulled the shirt sleeve off my arm. Walking around behind me with the shirt, she started bringing the sleeve down my injured right arm.

"Hmm, nasty, this may hurt a bit," she said, gently pulling the tattered fabric out of the crusty blood.

Damn, it hurts a lot. Don't cry baby. Tough this out. Thankfully, there was not a button left on my right cuff to interfere, but pulling the blood-soaked fabric free of the mangled flesh and scabs—oh my arm stung like hell. I was surprised by the number of pieces of road gravel that fell to the floor as she pulled the fabric from the scabs on my arm.

Interesting, feels better now that's it's bleeding again. Making a mess on the floor.

Finally, the shirtsleeve was free of my arm. Holding the remains of the shirt in two fingers, the nurse crossed to a shiny white can, stepped on the pedal at the bottom, the top opened and she dropped the shirt in, followed by the pair of rubber gloves she was wearing. The lid closed with a click as she crossed to a box of rubber gloves pulling on a fresh set. She stood next to the table under the large X- ray generator.

"Come here please."

I stepped over to where she stood next to the machine.

"Place your arm up here on this table."

Easy for you to say. I've had it bent across my stomach for hours. Not sure I can put it straight out. "What about the blood getting on the machine?" I asked, stalling for time as I gingerly tried to lift and open my arm. *Can't do it. Hurts too much.*

"The orderly will take care of that. Let me help you." Her gloved hand closed on my wrist firmly and none too gently pulled my arm across the table, lining it up with marks on the table. *Holy Jesus, Joseph, and Mary lady. Thought you were here to stop pain.* The cool X-ray table felt good on my throbbing arm.

"Don't move now," she said, stepping away and picking up a heavy lead lined apron, that as she donned it, it covered her from neck to knees. *Why don't I get one of those? My boys still work, your ovaries finished up years ago. Geez my arm hurts.* Buzz.

Hanging up the apron, she pulled the heavy film plate out from under my arm, stepping to the door and opening it, dropped it into a small box attached to the hallway side of the door. "Come with me please."

Holding my jacket in my left hand I followed her into the hallway once again and we headed back the way we came. She opened another door and led me in.

"Jump up on the table," she said., pulling a single step out from under the table.

I wonder if anyone has ever actually jumped onto the table. Remember how surprised the dentist was that time he said "Spit" and Clint did, right in his face. Dr. Bean handled it well. Clint's first visit. He didn't know about the spit bowl.

"Should I lay down?" I asked her as she loaded things out of the cabinets and drawers onto an adjustable height tray on wheels.

"No, I think sitting up will be best."

Rats. I'm kind of tired; could use a nap.

She returned and said, "Give me your arm."

I winced as I opened my elbow so she could examine my arm. She didn't examine it but took my arm firmly and stretched it out.

Oh damn that hurts. What are you doing to me?

"We need to debride your wounds. You can afford all this?" She said, reading my mind and asking a question I hadn't considered.

"Sure," I said confidently. *Mom and Dad's Blue Cross has always worked.* She used her free hand to begin working a solution of some kind into my gravel-filled arm. *Disinfectant? Geeze that burns like hell. Be careful; she reads minds. Dad said if it doesn't hurt, it's not working. Oh God help me.* I involuntarily tried to pull my arm back, but she pulled it back into position and continued the torment.

"This has to be done."

Yeah, I know, but what about a local. What's debride mean, Canadian for torture? My left hand probably left fingerprints in the treatment table, I was gripping it so tightly. With each stroke of her swab, gravel and sand fell into the white porcelain coated tray she had placed beneath my arm. Pain stabbed up my arm and neck exploding in my brain. *Smells like alcohol, hurts worse than all the mercurochrome Mom ever swabbed on my knees. If I faint, it will be really humiliating. Crying would be worse. She's not very big, wonder if she can catch me if I fall off the table. Oh, please let it be over—*

"All done. Now that wasn't so bad, was it?"

Afraid if I answer, I'll break into tears. Through clenched teeth, I managed to say, "Not too bad." *Liar.*

She gave me a strange uncomprehending look. "Well, just hold it up there, and I'll get it bandaged." She turned away to collect various items she would use for dressing the wounds.

I released the death grip I had on the table as the evaporating disinfectant cooled my wounds. They did feel better now that she wasn't digging the dirt and loose flesh out. As she dressed the wound, she gave me instructions on keeping it clean and when to change the dressing. She was interrupted by a knock on the door and the door simultaneously opening as a young man in a white coat walked in with an X-ray in his hand.

Why did he knock? Politeness? Didn't wait for an answer?

"Your arm isn't broken." *Good.* "How's the abrasion?"

Before I could answer, the nurse said, "It's clean and debrided. Should heal fine—"she turned her head away from the doc and looked at me "—if he follows instructions."

Yes. ma'am! No, she's doing a good job. no reason to be a smart ass. "I will. It feels a lot better already. Glad to know it's not broken."

"Okay. Then he can be discharged."

Rats, was hoping for an overnight for observation in a clean, warm bed. Tent is getting damp already. All this rain.

The nurse leads me back to the front counter that now had a middle-aged woman in street clothes sitting at it.

"He's ready to go," the nurse said, handing her a piece of paper.

"Hi," she said with a smile. "What's your medical number? Eh?"

"Err, don't have one, I'm not Canadian. Here's my insurance card." "Oh dear. We can't bill U.S. insurance." She opened a thick binder filled with printed pages and began going through.

Oh dear. She sounds like it will be hundreds. Thought Canada had cheap health care. Wonder how many days I'll have to empty bedpans?

"I'm afraid it all comes to twenty dollars. I'll give you an itemized receipt for your insurance, but I'll have to have payment now."

Or what, you'll call the Mounties? I looked at the bill: X- ray, ten dollars, debriding wound, five dollars, dressing wound, five dollars, total twenty dollars. "Do you take travelers' checks?"

"In U.S. currency?"

"Yeah."

"No, I can't take U.S. It must be Canadian."

I was checking my wallet. *Gotta get these greenbacks out and get some more of that colorful Canadian cash.* "Good news, I still have a twenty." I pulled the blue and white note with a portrait of Queen Elizabeth from my wallet. Handing it to the woman. *That's the end of my Canadian money, must cash a traveler's check.*

"Good, that covers it. Please give me the receipt for a moment." I handed it back. She stamped it *paid*, then handed it back to me. "Good day."

"You have a nice day too. Please thank everyone for me. Bye." I turned and walked out the door into the increasingly gloomy day as the clouds had sealed off the sky. I walked across town. *Wonder if I'll make it before it rains?*

CHAPTER THREE

BARFLY

The next morning, I pulled my clothes into my sleeping bag and got dressed. Getting dressed in a sleeping bag is a skill I perfected camping with Boy Scout Troop 93. Mr. Coon, our scoutmaster, insisted we would be warmer if we undressed before getting in the bag, because of the sweat that had collected in our clothes. He was right, but getting dressed—or undressed—in a cold tent was uncomfortable. We learned to do both while in the sleeping bag. It's awkward but surprisingly simple once you get the hang of it.

My bruised and wounded arm made me change from left arm first to right arm. I painfully managed to get my shirt on. Unzipping the tent flap, I looked out at a gloomy overcast day, thankful that the rain had stopped.

Jim's tall, skinny form was huddled over the struggling campfire. I crawled out and reached back in for my jacket, stood, and leaned forward, shrugging my shoulders to let me get the sleeve onto my damaged arm. Jim remained huddled over the fire.

"Are you trying to cook yourself for breakfast?"

He jumped in surprise. "How could you sleep? I was freezing in my tent and bag; I came out here and tried to build up the fire and get warm, but all the wood is wet. I'm still cold."

"A good morning to you too. Where's Dave?" I greeted him.

"Still asleep; you guys were both snoring so loud I couldn't sleep."

"I thought you couldn't sleep because you were cold," I teased.

"Damn it, it was both. Most miserable night of my life!" The usually mild-mannered Jim was pissed off.

"Shush, you'll wake Dave!" I kidded.

"I don't fucking care if I wake him up. Why should he sleep and keep me awake?"

"Hey, what's going on out here?" A bleary-eyed, red bearded face poked out of Dave's tent.

"Jim's having a temper tantrum because we kept him from his beauty sleep with our snoring," I answered.

Jim stormed off towards the gas station as Bear (Dave's nickname) crawled out of his tent in red wool long johns, with a seat flap and everything. As he scratched under his arms, I began peeling small strips of wood off a stick and tossing the kindling into the fire. They were small and thin enough that they burned well even though they were damp. I soon reached deep enough into the branch that I hit the dry heartwood. My mechanical method of drying resulted in the fire building up nicely. Dave carried his clothes over from the tent and dressed in the warmth of the renewed fire.

"I really need a cup of java. Shall we go find old sourpuss and hit the café for breakfast or should I fire up the stove and cook here?"

"We still have anything to cook?" Dave asked me.

"Coffee and some freeze-dried suppers. I think I'd rather have bacon and eggs in a warm café."

"Sounds good to me. Let's head off, grumpy," Dave said.

We caught up with Jim as he was leaving the station. El Coyote was still parked off to the side; I decided there was no point in asking if they had looked at it yet. We had the lumberjack's special: hash browns, toast, two eggs, and ham or bacon. Figured it would last us all day. I've never checked, but my father, a veteran of years on the road eating in restaurants, maintained breakfast was the best deal of the day. After soaking up all the coffee we could handle, we took care of our morning toilet in their restroom, then crossed the street to the station.

The mechanic was in and told me he was backed-up and wouldn't have time to look at the Land Cruiser for a couple of days. Depending on the diagnosis, if he needed parts, they would have to come from Prince Rupert, which would take a few days.

We returned to the campsite. I fired up my stove and made a pot of coffee. While I was occupied with the stove and coffee pot, Jim and Dave sat on a log discussing the situation. The coffee perking up into the viewer on the top of the pot was a rich dark brown. I grabbed the handle and announced, "Coffee's ready," as I poured a steaming mug full.

As I joined them on the log, Jim said, "How can you drink more coffee after all that you had at breakfast? You're a hopeless addict."

"That's why I want to go to South America where it's from."

"Yeah, about the trip," Dave said, "sounds like it could be at least a week before the car's fixed. Jim and I thought instead of sitting here getting moldy we would start hitching our way. Then when you catch-up to us, you could pick us up."

Staring into my coffee, I considered the change in plans. "Yeah, guess that could work. If you guys stay on the route we planned."

"Great. We just wanted to be sure you were okay with it," Jim said, jumping to his feet.

"Yeah. Better get going, we're burning daylight," Bear added as he headed for his tent.

I watched the two of them pack as I nursed my arm and sipped my coffee. During my third cup, they had their tents rolled up and tied to their packs. The colorful rain guards over their packs brightened the campsite. They helped each other get the packs on. Then they walked over to me.

I stood and said, "Well I'll see you down the road then."

"Yeah, feel bad about leaving you, but waiting around in this cold and wet is too much. Here, we thought we'd give you this to help with the repairs," Jim said, handing me a wad of bills.

"Thanks, I should be alright, Mom gave me a credit card to use in emergencies. Never needed it, but I guess getting the car fixed in Stewart qualifies if I run out of money. But this will help, thanks."

We all said, "see yah down the road", shaking hands, and they headed out. I sat back down and finished the pot of coffee and a chapter in the book I was reading.

Another cold rain started; I retreated to my little pup tent, which was so low I couldn't sit up in it. I lay down with my feet under the door flap to keep my muddy wet boots outside. I read on my back for a while, then I read on my stomach.

This tent was advertised as a two-man tent. I got it thinking I could take girls camping. That never happened. If it ever happens, we will be snug. To hell with this. I'm going to find someplace warm.

I opened the tent flap and crawled out into the rain. Quickly I grabbed my bib rain pants off the branch where I had hung them and hopped in, then quickly pulled on the raincoat. I avoided getting really wet; even the short walk to town caused my rain gear to absorb my body heat and I began warming up. I quickly walked past the few small businesses on main street. I had hoped but not really expected to find a library or something where I could sit and read in comfort.

I walked back to the gas station and climbed into El Coyote; at least I had a dry cushioned seat out of the wind and rain. I'm uncertain how long I read, but I noticed activity seemed to be increasing at the tavern that was part of the hotel's main floor.

I've always wondered about the people like my father who hang out in the bar as soon as it opens. I suppose if I nurse a beer, they won't object to me reading or writing a letter at one of the tables.

I crossed the street and entered the poorly lit but nicely appointed tavern: lots of dark wood word and red vinyl upholstery. I hung my rain gear on the hooks in the entryway and walked in. My wool shirt and jeans fit in with the dress code; my briefcase, even though tan corduroy with leather trim, didn't fit.

I found the smallest table, sat down, and started reading. I was quickly interrupted by an attractive waitress asking what I would like. I ordered a draft and sat reading, sipping my beer, and occasionally scanning the room to do a little people watching. I caught up on my letters and postcards to family and friends.

I kept nursing a beer, as one became empty, I would have another. I wondered if I was spending as much on beer as a hotel room would cost, but never got around to checking on that. The tavern quit serving at midnight. Then the staff started cleaning up to encourage those of us who were still there to drink up and get out. I think I was the last one out. The rain had stopped, and I stumbled home to my tent.

Good thing I'm not driving. I can barely walk. But I finally closed a bar.

The next day was pretty much a repeat of the day before. Use the restroom at the station, cross the street for the lumberjack's special where I read and drank coffee in the café until they asked me to leave. Then read sitting in the car until the tavern opened.

My arm improved and was almost back to normal by the third day, when I got the good news that they had figured out El Coyote's problem. The timing gear had broken in the landing. This seemed odd, but since I had worn one out my freshman year, it was a familiar problem. I cursed Toyota for using a synthetic gear instead of steel as I had the first time.

They ordered a new one, which of course wasn't available in Prince Rupert, and had to be shipped from a Toyota dealer in Vancouver, which would add at least an extra day to its arrival. At least, I had a grievance to drown as I spent the afternoon and evening drinking beer. I discovered you could get items off the café menu in the bar, so I added a burger and fries to my daily diet.

My third or fourth day, one of the regulars who sat with a group of men at one of the larger tables asked me to join them. I told my tale to the group, and we all began swapping stories. About closing time, the fellow who had invited me (I'm sorry I have forgotten your name) asked me if my arm could handle some work.

"Yeah, I think so. What did you have in mind?"

Don explained. "I'm a salvage logger. I'm putting together a raft of my logs down in the harbor for sale. If you have some waders, I could use a hand pulling the raft together."

"Never done anything like that, but I always enjoy a new experience. I have hip boots with me, will they do?"

"Yep. I'll pick you up at the café tomorrow morning about nine. Tide should be coming in then, so we can pull the logs into a raft."

"Great. See you then."

CHAPTER FOUR

❦

A MORALITY TEST

The next morning, I was waiting outside the hotel's café with my hip boots instead of my briefcase. A rather sorry looking Corolla pulled up. The rear suspension was shot, making the car look like it was always going uphill. Don called me over with: "Good morning. Hop in."

I opened the passenger door and discovered it was loose and sagged when it was open; to close, you had to lift and pull the door shut simultaneously. "Good morning. I was expecting a pick-up."

"Naw, we came up in the boat and bought this to get around town. Pick-up is down in Vancouver."

We made the short trip to the waterfront. Then Don pulled off the parking area and took a rough trail a hundred yards along the beach. We stopped at a small intertidal cove that was filling with water from the incoming tide; Don's logs haphazardly stored there were beginning to float.

We pulled on our waders and rain gear, wading out to the logs. Following Don's instructions, we began moving the logs into rows alongside each other. We fastened the logs together with a rope passed under and over the log. When we had eight logs tied into a raft, we moved it out to a dolphin: a large piling driven securely into the bottom, just beyond the low tide line.

The first raft was connected to the dolphin with a loop so the raft could rise and fall with the tide. Then we repeated the process, attaching the finished raft to the first. The length of the first raft enabled us to attach it first despite the deepening water as the tide came in.

Don had a small skiff on shore we could use if the water reached the top of our waders, but the shallowness of the cove and the length of the rafts let us stay in water shallow enough that we never launched the boat.

Wadding in the water and wrestling logs kept us warm until we were finished. The tide was still coming in, so we were in the water less than six hours, but the cold ocean water had robbed us of a lot of heat.

When we finally got out of the waders and back in the car, we were both shivering and starving to death. Don cranked the heat up to high, turned around, and headed for town. Through chattering teeth, he said, "That's done; let's get lunch." My only reply was my chattering teeth.

The drive to town, and the hotel café, was too short for the engine to warm enough for any heat to reach us. We both bailed out of the car, staggering into the café; our cold muscles just couldn't respond steadily.

"We need coffee," Don said as we slid into a booth. He ordered steak and eggs, which include hash browns and toast.

I chattered out, "The same please." My concern for the expense was relieved when Don added, "My treat."

As I guzzled coffee, we were joined by a small and very pretty woman and two small children. Don introduced everyone: Wendy, his wife, and Gail, his daughter, a much younger, golden-haired version of her mother, like seems to happen to all of us blonds—our hair darkens with age. The little boy, Dirk, was obviously his father's son, same stocky build, and blond hair. (Sorry, my memory and notes don't include the family's real names.) Following the introductions, Don said, "Have you guys eaten?"

"Yes, we had lunch on time. The kids can't wait."

"Sorry, but with Kim's help, the logs are all rafted and ready to be towed to town."

"Are you paying him?" Wendy sounded concerned. I wasn't sure if it was for me, or what paying me might do to the bottom line of Don's operation.

"I work cheap. I volunteered for the experience. Next time I'll charge more than just lunch," I chimed in.

"Good God, he owes you more than lunch! Look at you guys, you're still shivering, and I'm almost embarrassed to be sitting with two such dirty men."

She was thinking of me, that's nice.

Don swallowed a bite of toast and jelly, "We do need showers; Kim is living in a tent. After breakfast we can go back to the motel and he can use the shower."

"You're living in a tent? That must be terrible in this cold and rain. Don, I think there's room at the motel. The kids could camp on the floor and Kim could sleep in the hideaway."

"That's kind, but the shower will be plenty." *Sleeping bag is getting a bit damp and drying it out would be nice, but motel rooms aren't that big.*

"No, she's right. The kids will love camping on the floor, and you need to dry out."

"Okay, but the kids stay in the bed. A warm, dry floor will beat the wet ground." *Not putting the kids out; I remember resenting that when I was a kid.*

A couple hours later, a clean, warm, and dry Kim was on the floor of the motel playing Candy Land with the two children. The TV was on the CBC evening news, which I was watching and listening to while playing the game. It was nice to get caught up with what was going on in the world, but things hadn't really changed much in the couple of weeks since I had last listened to the news.

Don came out of the bedroom in slacks and a nice shirt. I'd never seen him out of work clothes, and he was almost unrecognizable. He sat on the couch saying, "Thanks again for babysitting, poor woman has been trapped in here by the rain with the kids for days now. A night on the town is going to do us both a world of good."

"No problem, I'm an old hand at babysitting, and the shower and being warm and dry is paradise after the tent. Parts for the Land Cruiser are supposed to be here today or tomorrow. Depending on how long the repair takes, I should be on the road soon."

Wendy stepped out of the bedroom in a short, tight skirt and matching top. She did a little twirl for Don, but I got the full benefit of it too. *Lucky bastard, bet he gets laid big time tonight.*

Don said, "Nice babe."

"Glad you like it. First chance I've had this trip to wear this outfit."

Don was up and holding her raincoat for her.

She looked at me, "You and the kids seem to be hitting it off." Switching her gaze, she added, "Now, you kids be good. If Kim gives me a good report, there might be an ice cream tomorrow." Stepping to the door Don was holding open, she continued, "Thanks for babysitting, I hope they behave."

As they parted, I said, "They're great; we won't have any trouble. Enjoy yourselves."

The children went down at their bedtime with no problem. I read for a couple of hours in the dark room with just a small reading lamp I had moved to the floor. My Thermorest had dried out quickly; the sleeping bag was taking a little longer. The inside was dry, but the outside was still damp, so when I finally closed my book, I only had my legs under the sleeping bag which doubled as a comforter. The hard work earlier made sleeping easy. Don and Wendy didn't wake me when they came in.

The next morning, Don needed to fly to Vancouver to arrange a tug for getting the rafts of logs to the mill. I volunteered to take care of the children, and Wendy drove him to meet the Grumman Goose that served as Stewart's connection to the outside world.

It was a nice day. It wasn't raining; fall is damp and cold in Stewart, and the children and I were able to play outside after they finished their breakfast. The small motel parking lot quickly lost its appeal, and so we walked downtown to window shop. We stopped at a variety store that had a children's pinball machine. They quickly exhausted my change. Gail was quite good, but Dirk played not much better than me; I never did master pinball.

We saw Wendy having coffee with some friends through the hotel's dining room window, and she waved us in. The kids got hot chocolates and I joined the table for coffee. Wendy asked, "Kim, the girls are going out tonight. All our husbands are out of town. Do you mind watching the kids again?"

"That's fine. If it's okay, I'll leave the kids with you right now and go check on the car repairs and my camp. Thought I'd pick up my dirty clothes and head to the laundromat."

"Thank you, that will work fine. You can use the laundry room at the motel; you're a guest there now, and they don't charge."

"Thank you, that's great. Nice meeting all of you." I got up and left, walking across the street to the service station. The parts were in, and they thought they would get to El Coyote later that day or the next. The tent was still standing, but the rainfly was soaked through, which meant the tent was starting to soak up water too. It just wasn't designed for the temperate rainforest.

Some of the guys at the bar had showed me pictures of Stewart in the winter, with snow so deep the roads almost looked like tunnels, with walls of snow eight and ten feet deep. Glad I was getting out before the snow flew in.

Laundry done, I carefully rolled everything tightly and packed it away in the pack. I left the bare essentials for two days in my day pack, which I hoped would be enough to get me out of town.

Gail, Dirk, and I were playing Chutes and Ladders when Wendy came out of the bedroom in a peasant blouse and swirling short dress, which showed off her nice shape and legs to full advantage.

Don is a lucky guy.

She knelt and kissed the kids, again warning them to behave. Thanking me again, she put on her jacket and headed out to meet the girls. I got really tired of Chutes and Ladders, even if it was a welcome change from Candy Land. I was very grateful when bedtime arrived.

With Don gone, the children got a special treat of sleeping with Mom, so I put them down in the master bedroom. After the late news, I spread my sleeping bag out on the hide-abed and crawled underneath.

I snapped awake when my chest was suddenly compressed under a warm, soft, but firm body. *Huh!* A hot wet tongue swirled into my ear, sending excited singles throughout my body. I couldn't see through all the hair on my face and mumbled into the cheek covering my mouth, "Whose it?"

The tongue left my ear as the weight on my chest lessened as Wendy raised her face a couple of inches above mine.

"Don, the damn bastard, is down there fucking the brains out of his girlfriend. I'm going to show him two can play that game. Get ready to have your world rocked."

She couldn't have seen him with his girlfriend. How does she know? Thou shall not commit adultery, especially with your friend's wife! Get out of here!

As Wendy's face dropped to mine again, I gently pushed her off onto the bed as I slipped off over the edge.

"Wendy, you're a babe and I'll probably regret not screwing you, but Don and you are my friends and it's wrong to sleep with you." I picked up my pants from the chair and slipped into them as I spoke.

Wendy writhed seductively on the hide-a-bed, patting the bed next to her, "He's cheating on me. It's okay if I cheat on him. You're going to miss one hell of a ride."

I had started stuffing my sleeping bag into its sack. "Wendy we would both hate ourselves in the morning. What if one of the kids wakes up and comes in?" *Appealing to motherhood should slow her down. Damn she looks good, what does the song say, "love the one you're with"? That doesn't include your friend's wife.* The distraction of the sound of her nylons rubbing on her legs, her writhing and patting the bed, distracted me. I stood there with two-thirds of the sleeping bag in the stuff sack, wrestling with temptation. She knew it and continued her seductive motions.

"Come on, baby," she purred, patting the bed. "Help me show that bastard."

"No. He's my friend, and you're his wife." I pulled on a flannel shirt, leaving it open. Grabbed my day pack and stepped into my boots. My heels didn't make it, they were on top of collapsed leather of the boot's ankles.

As I fumbled with the doorknob's lock, she jumped up on to her hands and knees, "You better fuck me because I'm telling Don you did whether you do or not! You may as well have some fun before he beats you to a pulp."

I looked back at her as I closed the door. The soft *come hither* look on her face had disappeared as she threatened me. Her previously pretty face was now a hard and narrowed-eyed, the look of a vicious demon.

I closed the door, hobbling away, my boots half on, my hands and arms full of my possessions, and a cold wind and misty rain blowing through my open shirt, cutting right through my tee, and chilling my skin.

Nothing like a cold shower to turn off lust. Made the right choice I'm sure, but she had a point. If I'm going to take a beating either way, maybe I should have enjoyed myself. She does look like a hot fuck. Kim, Hemingway said a moral act is one you feel good about afterwards and immoral is one you feel bad about. In this case I am sure I would have felt bad. Geez, I'm getting cold. Better finish dressing. Going to rain.

I stopped, pulling up my boots and tying them. *Probably should have done the shirt first. I'm starting to shiver.* I finished buttoning my shirt and pulled on my jacket and raincoat. *All right, everything is shipshape. Wonder if I'll ever get to go out to sea in this job. Doing the Yukon by boat was cool, but I grew up navigating rivers; I'd like to try the ocean.*

Almost to the station, wonder if they left El Coyote outside? Might be warmer than the tent. You walked away from a warm bed, Kim. Yeah, but I can still look myself in the mirror.

Nope, rig is locked up in the bay. At least they're working on it. Maybe, I can leave town before Don gets back. Wonder if he's really cheating. Damn it's dark, wonder if I can find the trail to the tent?

"Fuck!"

A wet branch slapped my face as I missed the trail in the dark. My thoughts continued randomly as I reached the clearing; even in the dark, the tent looked wet and uninviting. *Damn, you pride yourself on your woodman's ship. Get tough.* I climbed in the wet door, unrolled the Thermorest.

At least it's dry, good thing you had stuff ready to go, almost like you knew you'd have to run. Nah, I was just making space for kids and me. I cheated and gave the valve a gentle puff of air. *I'm getting cold, but didn't want to wear that wet rain gear into here, Damp enough without me dragging in more water. Now get out of your clothes. Remember what*

Mr. Coon taught you and you learned the hard way, sleeping in your clothes just makes you colder.

As I shivered in the sleeping bag, warming it up with my body heat, my mind went back to that hot piece of ass I walked away from, then I remembered Marie, and many other failed relationships as I fell back into my interrupted sleep.

CHAPTER FIVE

NO ESCAPE

The next day, I slipped back into my tent life routine, heading to the service station washroom to brush the night off my teeth.

They told me they were working on the Land Cruiser and expected to be finished later that day. I spent the morning and afternoon mostly in the café soaking-up coffee, eating my meals, and getting snacks so I wouldn't be asked to leave. After supper, I went into the bar and ordered a pitcher of beer, expecting the usual drinking companions to join me when they got off work. I lit my pipe, opened my book, and settled in for an evening of nursing a beer so I could stay warm and dry until closing.

Don surprised me when he was the first to join me. He was very angry, the tension in his body and expression on his face told me I had seconds to live.

Just one step closer to the door, please. Alabama's song echoed in my head.

Through clenched teeth, Don hissed, "I've heard her story. Before I kill you I want to know your side."

Thanks for the chance. Will the truth work? I didn't rehearse any lies. Truth is it.

I repeated the events of last night, with some edits to improve Wendy's actions.

Don visibly began relaxing during my story. "Well, nice of you to be so kind in your description of the jealous bitch. I didn't think you were the kind of person who would screw another man's wife when the kids were in the next room. I don't know what I'm going to do with her.

The next time she'll probably pick up some guy in the bar looking for a piece. Then we both will be screwed. She just doesn't understand I can't be home every night and make a living. Oh well, it's not your problem." He flagged down the waitress and ordered another pitcher and a glass. "Still friends?" he extended his hand, which I took saying, "Of course."

"Sorry to kick you out into that wet tent. Any idea how long till you leave?"

"Sounds like with a little luck, they'll be done tomorrow."

"Well, at least there's some good news," Don said.

Some of our lumberjack friends were off work and joined us. They ordered meals; the café also served in the bar. Wendy didn't come up again as we told stories and drank beer. The people at the table changed as some joined other friends at another table or went home. Don was one of the latter.

Looking at his back as he left, I thought, *Take it easy on her. Strange as it seems, it's because she loves you she acted out. Hope they can work things out.*

The waitress came around. "Last call, either finish what you have or order one more. We're closing." Her tone clearly indicated she was tired and wished we would all go home. My home was a damp cold tent. I asked the last two guys left at the table, "Ready for one more?"

I had interrupted this big dark-haired guy who was telling us about his new four by four pick-up and how he was customizing it.

"Yeah, ugh," he said, looking at the other guy who was draining his glass.

Smacking his lips, he said, "Sure."

I ordered another pitcher; I really didn't want to go to the tent. The waitress gave me a look that could kill, but she brought the pitcher.

As tables emptied, she wiped them off, putting the chair on them upside down. The bartender washed and dried glasses, putting them away under the bar. Then when we were the only ones left, and all the tables were covered with chairs, he told the waitress to go home. "I'll close up when this bunch finishes."

"Hey, have you been Hyderized yet?" the big guy with the pick-up said to me.

"No, but it's too late. The border is closed."

"That's not a problem, nobody watches who comes and goes after they close. Let's go, these people want to go to bed, but the night is still young and they know how to drink in Alaska."

It was a short trip to the border; Stewart, B.C., and Hyder, A.K. are linked by a huge gold and silver mine on the border of Alaska and Canada. The ore is trucked out of the mountains through Hyder into Stewart, where it is loaded on boats. Getting Hyderized is a tradition arising from the local Everclear; a shot or two will get the hardest drinker drunk, or in our case, drunker.

The border was closed when we arrived; we drove through without slowing down. We went through some scattered cabins and arrived at Hyder's saloon. Our driver took the microphone off his dash, switched to speaker, and ordered three as we parked. We walked inside to find our three shots set-up on the bar. The driver said, "See what a time saver that's going to be?"

We bellied up to the bar and toasted Hyder's late closing hour. Being no stranger to Everclear, I wasn't surprised by the breathtaking burn as it went down my throat.

The bearded bartender explained the tradition of newcomers signing and dating a bill, then stapling it to the wall. I unsteadily walked over and began reading the wall. There were a few unexpected celebrity names, but the only one I remember was Bing Crosby. My companions called me over for a second round. The third was mine to buy. Being cheap, I remember I signed and dated a Canadian dollar bill (This was

before Looneys and Tunney's.). After an afternoon and evening of beer and three Everclear, things had become a bit fuzzy. I assume the dollar made it to the wall.

My next memory was our driver pulling up onto a yard in Stewart. He pulled-up with the fender touching the corner of the house. "My damn renters are months behind on their rent. Maybe this will get em out.

All four wheels began spinning, tearing up the grass in the yard, but other than the roar of the barely muffled engine, nothing happened. "That didn't work, let's see how strong this steel is." (He had replaced the standard bumper with a piece of steel beam.) He backed up a few feet, then floored the accelerator.

CRASH.

My teeth rattled in my mouth. We backed up and saw people come running out the front door.

"Better get out of here." Our driver fled. I assume he dropped me near my campsite because I woke up cold and damp in the tent, seriously hungover. I stumbled through my morning routine. I was shivering as I walked past the station, but El Coyote was still in the shop. Rather than stopping, I continued on to the café, using their restroom to scrub the night off my teeth. My stomach was still a little queasy. I skipped the heavy breakfast and just had toast and coffee. Lots of coffee.

Feeling almost human, I crossed the street to check on the L.C. status. Hallelujah! The garage door was open, and El Coyote backed out into a parking place. I rushed into the office, and there was a blur of paperwork, signing travelers checks, and a last-minute filling of the tank. The best hangover cure ever is really good news.

I started the engine and marveled at the rumble of the straight six that I really hadn't expected to ever hear again. I pulled forward and cranked the steering wheel to the left to enter the street. The car continued forward, even with the wheel turned to the stop on the left. *Oh hell, now what?* I slammed my head into the steering wheel and sat there trying to get my brain to shift gears from elation to problem solving.

The door opening next to me, startled me as I turned, and looked into the mechanic's face.

"What's wrong?" he asked.

"Can't turn left. It's cranked over all the way to the stop."

He muttered an obscenity under his breath. "Back it up, we'll get it back into the shop." He walked back to the garage.

I put the car in reverse and backed up past the pumps and the open garage door. Which, fortunately, put the door to the right of the L.C., the direction it would turn. I pulled in over the hoist and climbed out.

The crew gathered around under the car, checking on everything they could think to check. I resisted the temptation to join them and put in my two cents and instead sat in the public reception area in an uncomfortable little chair, drinking the terribly weak coffee from their big coffee maker.

"Bad news," the mechanic announced his arrival. *Now what?* "Your frame is bent. There aren't any frame straightening equipment until you get to Vancouver. I've got the guys realigning your front end. With a little luck, you'll be able to steer well enough to get to where you can have the frame straightened."

"I've been a little short of luck lately." *Not true, Don believed you.* "I'll cross my fingers," I said to the mechanic's back as he turned to return to the shop.

A few minutes later, I heard El Coyote start-up. The mechanic backed it out and drove in a circle around the gas pumps to the left and right to check the steering.

Fucking A! It works, old Coyote looks like crab on the straightaway, but I'll watch for weird tire wear. Wonder how many times I'll need to rotate tires between here and Des Moines. Dad will know someone to straighten the frame. Wonder how that's done?

"There she is, turns right and left, you're all set," the mechanic said as he came in the front door.

"Yeah, I saw. What do I owe you?"

"Nothing. We got enough of your money already. Have a good trip," he said as I stood with my hand out. We shook.

"Thank you, and tell the crew thanks. I'm off!" I climbed into the L.C. *All in all, nice people here, but I'm sure glad to be on the road. Guess I'll head home and get the frame straightened, then see if I can find June down in Austin.*

I put in my eight track of the Carpenters and headed out of town singing. Luckily, El Coyote was not a music critic. Until my voice changed, I used to regularly sing solos in the youth choir at church.

BANG!

My foot automatically floored the clutch as I turned towards the right shoulder. My vision was obscured by oil spreading over the windshield. I turned off the engine and coasted to a stop alongside the road. *Fuck, damn, shit, what is it now?*

I got out to appraise the damage. The oil on the windshield had obviously come up through the vent to the engine compartment. The side vents also had oil spray that spread down the side of the car to the rear wheels. *Never seen anything like this. Did I blow a head gasket or cylinder?*

I opened the hood; instead of propping it open, I waked it back and let it rest on the windshield. *What a fucking mess! Not going to be able to see anything till it gets' steam cleaned.*

I reached for the dipstick, but the handle was dripping oil. I got the roll of paper towels I kept under the front seat and returned to the oily dipstick. Using a tripled-up towel, I pulled the dipstick out, wiping it off with some others, then returned it to its hole. Pulled it out and checked the oil level, none showing. *Could this mess on the engine and car be a single quart? A little oil goes a long way.*

I got the extra can of oil I carry, and my can spout, and added the oil to the engine. Checked the oil level again, and there was still nothing showing. I noticed a large pool of oil forming in the gravel underneath the engine.

Shit. Well, that sure blows the first day with sunshine and good luck all to hell. Engine was still running when I coasted off the road and turned it off. It's not frozen. That's good news. Don't dare try starting it. The way oil is running out something is seriously wrong.

I continued studying the engine looking for the source of the oil. *Must have blown the short block gasket. Never heard of that, unless that's what people mean when they say, "blew the head". Worse, could've cracked the head. How long will it take to get one of those here? Kim, a good cry might help now. No, speaking of here, where is here?*

I checked my watch. It was about an hour and fifteen minutes since I left Stewart. *Let's see, probably averaged about fifty, been stopped for fifteen, so fifty miles.* I checked my map of B.C.; I wasn't even halfway to the next town. *Kim, you haven't seen a car or truck yet. Anyone who stops no matter which way, we're getting on.* I grabbed a book out of my day pack and settled into the driver's seat.

Not sure how long I waited. I finished several chapters, my thermos of coffee, and took several short walks. Finally, I heard an engine slowing, looked up, and a log hauler was stopping, headed towards Stewart.

I marked my place and was out the door before the truck stopped. Since I was standing next to the truck driver's door, he just rolled down his window and asked what the problem was. I told him it seemed I had blown something and all my oil was gone. He stepped out, took a look and said, "Let's load her up. I'll take you into Stewart. There's a service station there."

"Okay. They know me well, just spent a week there, waiting for parts."

Then we pushed El Coyote across the road to the back on his flatbed. He dropped a couple of loading ramps he had for loading equipment when he wasn't hauling logs, we lined them up with the wheels, he attached his winch cable and I drove the crippled beast as he winched it onto the truck. In no time, we were unloading the L.C. at the service station in Stewart. He wouldn't take anything for his trouble, not even lunch.

"Back again! What, shit, looks like you blew it up. She frozen?" The mechanic had arrived wiping his hands on a rag.

"Yeah, I only made it about fifty miles, then bang! I can't tell what blew through the mess. I got it shut down before it stopped, I don't think it's frozen."

"Let's push it over here, can't work on it for a couple of days."

"That's what I expected. You probably fell behind replacing my timing gear."

"Yep." He said as we parked the L.C.

I signed the work order to have the problem diagnosed. I was very down and stood there with my complimentary coffee trying to decide what to do next. A Canadian Mountie walked in, no, not the pretty red dress, ceremonial uniform, but the everyday blue.

"I got a moose, but I need some help getting it out, anybody want to help?"

He got congratulations on his successful hunt, but no offers of help. *Hell, it will give you something to do while you figure this mess out.* "Hi, I'm not doing anything. Is it okay for a nonresident to help?"

"I'm the law, so it's okay," he joked.

I followed him out to his truck. It was a little Mulligan bull, young and tender, just right for eating. It had dropped in a spot right where Frank (sorry I've forgotten his real name) could back right up to the moose. Frank jumped into overalls that had some blood on them, which explained how he gutted a moose without getting his uniform bloody.

Still didn't get much on the overalls. Have to admire a man who can keep clean doing such a messy job. Have to remember the overalls trick.

Even a small moose is big. By lifting the front half into the truck bed and tying it there to keep it from slipping back to the ground, we were able to lift the hind quarters up and push the whole moose into the bed.

The official Mountie residence included his home, office, and a large high ceiling garage. Frank backed into the garage. We tied the moose to a large hook in the ceiling. Frank pulled the truck out from under the moose, I stayed and caught the moose, stopping its swing. His wife and child came out into the garage to welcome him home with hugs and kisses. She asked him, "Can that wait until after supper?"

Their toddler was apprehensively approaching the moose. I dropped down to my knees on the floor next to the child and said, "The moose can't hurt you. You can pet it if you want."

Wide blue eyes looked at me, then turning to the moose, tentatively approached with an outstretched hand, I reached out stroking the moose's hair on the nearest front leg. The little hand followed my example; there was a squeal of delight and fear, and the little one ran back, grabbing its mother's leg.

She scooped the child up, saying, "You touched that dirty thing, you'll have to wash your hands before supper. Kim, you're welcome to join us."

After a great supper, we each took a side of the gutting incision, and began skinning while drinking beer. As I carried the hide out to the truck, Frank's butcher friend arrived and I carried in his meat grinder. Following the butcher's instructions, we disassembled the moose with our knives and bone saw. Then wrapped and labeled the cuts of meat grinding scraps and "waste" pieces.

We packaged everything in portions suitable for Frank's family of three, except for the portions the butcher set aside for his family. By midnight, the moose was cut, wrapped, and placed in the freezer, except tenderloins in the refrigerator for tomorrow's supper.

I finished a beer, *Hmm, don't really want to set up the tent tonight, sounds like it's pouring rain. Guess I'll just have him drop me at the hotel. Hard on the bank balance, but hell this trip is over. Guess I'll call Mom tomorrow. Dad's last words when we said goodbye were: "Remember you can always come home, son." Wonder what it costs to fly to Des Moines from here.*

"I think that can's empty. Do you want another?"

Lowering the can from my lips, I said, "Sorry, I was lost in thought for a moment. This has been fun. I learned a lot. Can you drop me at the hotel?"

"You have a strange idea of fun, but I'm glad you did; we'd still be butchering without your help. No hotel, we have a whole dormitory wing the government pays to maintain. You're welcome to stay."

"That would be great." *Don't say unnecessary, it would be stupid.* "I'll get my stuff." I went over to the corner where I had set my pack and sleeping bag and followed him through the house and into the dorm. "Wow, what's all this space for?"

"Extra Mounties, guess they worry Hyder will attack us."

We both laughed as he showed me into a room with steel bunk beds and a small desk. I unrolled my sleeping bag and spread it out over the chair at the desk so it could get the damp out. Slipped under the clean sheets and was asleep in minutes.

I had breakfast with the family the next morning and Frank dropped me at the station as he started his patrol. I told the mechanic my plan and left my contact information in Des Moines. I crossed the street to the café and had a cup of coffee while I read a book, then paid for it with twenty, getting all the coin they could spare for the pay phone call home. Did some time zone calculations, discovered I would have to wait till afternoon for Mom to get home from school.

Fell back on my old daily plan of drinking coffee and reading in the café until lunch. After lunch, a couple of more chapters and more caffeine. Finally, three o'clock arrived and I think I caught Mom walking in the door as the phone rang. I updated her on my situation.

She got the number of the pay phone so she could call me back, and I leaned against the wall next to the phone (it was in a hallway between the bar and café) reading. Finally, probably really was less than half an hour, Mom called back. I was ticketed all the way through and needed to start with the morning flight out of Stewart down at the dock. With that settled, I walked back to the Mountie station to pick-up my gear.

Frank's wife wouldn't hear of me leaving for a tent camp, so I helped with dinner, which mostly meant I entertained the toddler so she was free to work.

Another warm, dry night, and the next morning, Frank dropped me at the dock on the waterfront. I climbed into a Grumman Goose for the milk run to Prince Rupert.

The planes got progressively larger as I flew to Vancouver onto Calgary onto Minneapolis-Saint Paul, and finally Des Moines. Mom and Dad were at the airport, excited to see me. I was surprised my brother, Clint, hadn't changed the room, so I was able to watch Johnny Carson with my father and go to bed. Clint was out on a date. *Weird how this all seems normal when it's not.*

CHAPTER SIX

MARSHA

I had been home for Christmas a couple of years before, but there still were all the usual getting reacquainted and fitting into the household routines again. Part of which included me calling my high school friends to find out who was still around. Dan Porter and his wife, Laura, were home and eager to see me and my slides of Alaska. We settled on a day when I would come to supper.

The next day, while I was laying around the house (everyone else was at work) the phone rang.

"Hi, Kim, it's Laura."

"Hi, I was just getting ready to start on the Eskimo ice cream for dessert."

"I called because a class of dental techs from D.M.C.C. (Des Moines Community College) toured the lab today. One of the girls and I got to talking, and she said she was thinking of going to Alaska when she graduated because she's bored with Des Moines. I told her I had a friend from Alaska coming to supper on Wednesday and I would ask him if he would like to bring her. Would you like to?"

Think I got all the pronouns right, blind date! "What does she look like?"

"The usual, two arms, two legs. Great personality."

"Hmm." *Not much to look at. What the hell?* "Okay, what's her phone number?"

I wrote it down, Laura went back to work, and I began filleting a pike from the freezer. *Blind date, be a first for me. Plain is okay, hope she's not ugly, could just go without her and tell Laura she changed her mind. She has the phone number and might call to see why this Marsha cancelled.*

I made the special extra incisions in the filets to remove the pike's Y bones. A real pain and why my dad avoided cleaning pike. Not having boiled one before, I didn't realize I could remove the bones easily during the shredding process. Cutting the filets into thirds, I dropped them into a pot of salted water and turned on the heat, then crossed the floor to the breakfast nook and slid into the corner where the phone was. Looking at my note, I dialed the number. *Wonder if I'm calling too early? She might be in class, then I could say I didn't get an answer.*

A beautiful, smooth, sexy voice said, "Hello?"

Wow, what a hello, probably the beautiful sister. "Hi, is Marsha there?" I managed, sounding like an insecure eighth-grader.

"Yes, I am, who are you?" the voice replied with just a note of suspension.

"Hi, I'm Kim Francisco, you met my friend Laura at the dental lab today. She called and gave me your number and said you would be interested in seeing my slides of Alaska when I show them tomorrow." I rattled it off like a machine gun, except machine guns are no protection against women.

"Oh, I remember. The two of us were goofing off, talking. I missed most of the lab tour. Yes, I would like to come. I don't have a car. Can you pick me up?"

Geez, I hope so, you might be a three-hundred pounder for all I know. "Yes, my brother is letting me use his Pinto. I could pick you up at six if that's alright," continued my rapid-fire speech.

"You'll need to know where I live. It's a little hard to find."

Idiot, she doesn't sound like a dateless three-hundred pounder. Sounds like she's used to tongue tied, scared boys.

"Yes, of course. I have a pencil and paper right here." Mom and Dad always kept a notepad under the phone in the often-vain hope one of us kids would take a message.

"Okay, the address is 6709 Forest Court, in Clive. Do you know where St. Teresa's is on University?"

"No, how about from Merle Hay Mall?"

"Umm, take Merle Hay to Hickman, turn left on 63rd ah, used to driving it without noticing the streets—then right on Colby, then right onto 66th, then it's only a block or two to Forest Court, turn right. It's a brick, two story house with a dormer and a big tree on the right side. If you hit 69^{th,} you've gone too far. Do you have all that?" Marsha asked.

"Yes, been on Merle Hay to Hickman lots of times, that's how we get to the Chili King, best chili in Des Moines. The rest is new to me, but your directions seem clear enough. Is it okay to pick you up at six?"

"Yes, six will be fine. I'm looking forward to your slides."

"I hope they don't disappoint. I'm still an aspiring photographer."

"I'm sure they'll be great! I don't really know anything about Alaska. Bye!"

"Till tomorrow then. Bye." *Wow, I'm in love or lust or something with that voice, no chance her face and bod match, but with that voice she could be forgiven for a lot.*

I spent most of the rest of the evening trying to anticipate her questions and practicing smooth answers. The next morning, after breakfast, I drove Mom the short hop to Samuelson in her Pacer. Then looking at Marsha's directions, I headed to Merle Hay and Douglas, continued onto Hickman, all of which was familiar so I barely thought about it. At the turn onto 63rd, I had to start paying close attention and annoyed the drivers behind me as I drove slowly so I could read all the street signs, which was the reason for the practice run. I didn't want Marsha to think I was a dope who didn't know his way. Her directions were perfect as I slowly drove past the brick house.

Dad always says you can tell how intelligent a person is by their directions. Guess she must be smart along with having a hypnotic voice.

I picked up my mother at five o'clock that evening at the school. Workaholic that she was, I watched in amazement as she drew perfectly parallel lines free hand on the chalkboard for her first graders printing lesson the next day. Never understood how she did that. I have trouble doing straight lines with a straight edge. "You look nice,"

she said, as she collected her 'homework' for the evening from her desk.

"Yeah, showered, shaved, and trimmed the beard after I got my hair cut. Never met this girl before, but wanted to make a good impression. I think you taught me that."

"Not much of a haircut. Remember how nice you looked with a butch?"

"Mom, I was five years old," I replied. Our conversation on hair styles continued as I drove her home. I repeated my drive to Marsha's, but included a twist down 69th that was a little shorter. As I pulled Clint's standard shift Pinto (his car was behind Mom's) into the driveway, I noticed it ran downhill.

That's unusual, must cover the garage floor with water when it rains. All right stay calm, you're a man of the world now, not a scared eighth grader.

I confidently walked up the sidewalk to the front door, didn't see a doorbell, so knocked firmly, but not like it was a police raid. The door opened; I gulped as I was transported back to the eighth grade. The woman I was looking at had long, shoulder-length straight Peggy Lipton blonde hair, which like mine was darkening to dishwater blonde, but she still had some highlights. Her oval face was perfect. The tight orange sweater showed off her smallish frame, but perfectly in balance with her lean body and breasts. Next was a green miniskirt that displayed a pair of magnificent legs, even in the backlighting from the house.

"Hi, I'm Marsha. You must be Laura's friend."

Speak stupid! Just relax. "Hi Marsha, I'm Kim, err might be a little chilly for just the sweater." *Yes, mother, what's wrong with you? There's a coat over her arm.*

She took a step out, pulling the door shut behind her. "I think you're right," she said, as she put an arm into the coat. I quickly stepped around behind her, taking the coat and guiding it across her back and up where she could put her other arm in.

"Hey, our coats sort of match, except for the color." Her coat was red suede, mine was a dark brown suede.

As we walked towards the car, she looked at me saying, "Well, they are different styles." Hers was a trench coat style and mine was just a broad lapeled jacket.

As we reached the car, I said, "A woman would notice more than just the color. Usually, when I pick someone up, the father or family committee wants to meet me," I said, opening the passenger door. The Pinto was low, and as she slipped in with one hand on the hem of her skirt it still rode up, revealing even more perfect thighs. I was transfixed, impressed as she sat that they were so firm her weight caused hardly any expansion.

Stop staring.

Her lovely, small hand reached up for the door handle, pulling it towards her, breaking my stare, as she shut the door. *Idiot, why don't you just say I want to devour you. Hey, she is used to it. See how handily she used the door?*

As I was slipping into the driver's seat, she answered the question, "My dad died when I was thirteen, Mom's on a date, and my little sister is next door at the neighbors."

"Oh, I'm sorry about your dad." *Leave it to you to bring up a terrible memory. What a way to start a date.*

"That's okay, it was a long time ago. I'm twenty-one and can take care of myself. Fathers give you a bad time?"

About now, I had shifted the Pinto's manual transmission down into reverse, but as soon as I put the clutch in to shift, the car began rolling towards the garage door. I hit the accelerator and popped the clutch, killing the engine. *Shit.* "Sorry, first time driving my brother's car; I'm use to my gear shift, his seems more sensitive," I said, glad the darkness covered up my hot, red face.

"I don't even know how to drive a manual," Marsha assured me.

I tried again, trying to let the clutch out a little slower. The car started rolling towards the garage, the clutch engaged, and the car gave a shudder as I killed it once again. My face was on fire.

Swearing under my breath, my feet and hands repeated the process trying to use the memory of the earlier attempts to get the job done. Result was worse, sort of, the car started jumping backwards as I tried to give it enough gas to smooth the transmission' gear engagement. After about three hops up the driveway, it died again. "Fucking damn hill!

Oh, I'm sorry, I don't usually talk like that. It's just the hill and car are really embarrassing me."

"It's okay, I've heard worse, and especially after ice storms, the whole family has struggled with this driveway and all of our cars are automatic."

Her words were very comforting. I started the car again, and learning from my first three tries, I managed to feel the transmission and smoothly shift into reverse, backing out of the driveway and onto the street.

Dan and Laura lived back in the direction of my parent's home, on Hickman Road, one of Des Moines major arteries. We arrived, following greetings and introductions, we had supper. Then my day's labor making the akutaq, Eskimo Ice Cream.

I knew the ingredients from my summer in Emmonak, but not the proportions. Mrs. Mosses had told me it was made with Crisco, wild berries, flaked boiled fish, and sugar. I had spent the afternoon boiling and flaking the pike filets from my parent's freezer, then experimenting with small batches mixing the fish with Crisco, berries from the store, and sugar.

I discovered a number of things: domesticated berries are larger and blander than wild; wild blueberries are about a third of the size but have ten times the flavor of a tame one. Of course, I couldn't find crow berries, moon berries, or black berries (no relation to our black berry), so I substituted raspberry, blackberries, strawberries, and a personal favorite cherry. A little Crisco goes a long way when mixing it with fish flakes. Lastly but not least, sugar covers a multitude of sins.

I finally got a small batch that I liked, expanded the recipe using the proportions and mixing order I stumbled on a little Crisco, about three times as much flaked fish, as much sugar as Crisco and fish, then fold in all the berries you have. Mom had a can of "whipped cream dessert topping" in the fridge, which seemed to be a nice addition so I took it along.

I was munching happily away on mine, looking up while I chewed, I noticed the dessert topping was gone from everyone else's akutaq, but otherwise there didn't seem to be much interest. Marsha was picking out the berries. Laura's eyes met mine and she said, "I don't like fish." Dan just said what the rest were thinking, "Kim, you must have been really hungry. I don't like it."

"That's okay, probably an acquired taste. My feelings aren't hurt," I lied and collected everyone's plates and dumped them back into the bowl I brought it in.

Marsha said, "I liked the berries."

"I came prepared. I didn't bring bowls, but I left half-a- gallon of real ice cream in your freezer.

Laura, followed by Marsha, jumped to their feet, and went into the kitchen to serve the ice cream. Which was followed by my slides, which I didn't think were very good, but we all had fun watching and talking.

We went to a late movie, West World. After the lights went down, I tried the old 'stretch and let your arm end up over your date's shoulders move.' I blundered again and got my watch band tangled in Marsha's long hair. Smiling at me, she deftly took my arm, untangled her hair, then guided it around her neck as she leaned her head into my shoulder. To ensure my hand behaved, she intertwined her fingers in mine, resting the back of her hand on her breast, with my hand on top of hers. I was thrilled to be able to feel every breath she took.

Back at Laura and Dan's house, Marsha and I sat down on the floor, shoulder to shoulder, and began comparing histories, dreams, goals, values, and intersections of our lives. The main one being that before his death Marshal, her father, had been an actuary with an insurance company which used my great uncle as their physician. Marshal and George were friends, and we were able to compare our visits to the large house Dr. Waters and my great aunt, Alice, had.

We talked and kissed, talked some more, and necked some more. Suddenly, it was four o'clock in the morning. Dan and Laura had long before given up on us and gone to bed. I drove Marsha home and we made a date to meet the next day for lunch. I kissed her goodnight at the door and floated back to the car.

I think this is really the one, this time. Marsha's why all the others didn't work out. I'm hers to keep or throw back.

54

CHAPTER SEVEN

PROPOSAL

Luckily for me, Marsha was still completing her certification program as a dental assistant, otherwise I don't know how I would have done all the pheasant hunting I did that fall. Between our courtship, her classes, and my pursuit of ring necks, we both were sleep deprived.

One unusually warm day in November, just a couple of weeks after our first date, I took her for a picnic lunch at one of Des Moines City parks. I got to rattling on about the cabin I would build for us outside Fairbanks and what the next winter would be like. I finally ran down and paused for her to comment. Smiling, her brown eyes sparkling, she said "Haven't you forgotten something?"

Ugh, what did I forget, summer in Emmo, fall building cabin in Fairbanks, winter trapping unless I land a biologist job? "Err, I don't think so; I mean, I sort of assumed you would want to work for a dentist, but you don't have to."

Laughing harder, she rolled off her elbow onto her back and said, "Kim, when did you ask me to marry you? Did I say yes?"

I slapped my forehead so hard I gave myself a headache. "Well, err, will you?"

"Is that a proposal?"

"Not a very good one. I suppose now's not the right time. I kind of ruined the moment, didn't I?"

She sat up, throwing her arms around me, and said, "Yes, ask again in a few days." Then we fell back onto the blanket hugging and kissing.

CHAPTER EIGHT

RETURN PREPARATION

I had managed to fit in checking the newspaper want ads for another Land Cruiser every day, along with courting Marsha, pheasant hunting, and household chores. My grandmother had agreed to loan me the money with no interest, a good deal, but it still rankled a little, since she had given my sister and a couple of cousins her old cars rather than trading them in. I was pretty sure I had spent more hours doing yard and gardening work for her than the others, but she had always paid me, so I decided it just continued our employee/employer relationship. There was a twenty-five-hundred-dollar limit on the loan.

There weren't many L.C.s for sale, but finally, one day, I looked at one on the Eastside of Des Moines. It looked really good, but I had done all the maintenance for many years on El Coyote, so after the test drive, I crawled underneath, inspecting all the trouble areas for leaks and other problems. The owner was a little surprised at how long I was under the hood and car inspecting, but answered all my questions.

I finally just lay under the rig, thinking, *Seals are tight, oil plug tight, little bit of grease on bottom of clutch, but don't think I've seen an L.C. that didn't have that if it had more than ten-thousand miles. Shocks, springs, steering stabilizer are all tight. Wheel knuckles tight, brake shoes good on the one wheel I pulled. I think it's safe to skip others. Crankcase oil looked good, transmission oil looked good and filled to check hole. Antifreeze tested good and rad full. Rubber is pretty good, plugs clean, exhaust looks good. Can't think of anything else to look at. Only problem is he's asking for three-thousand and ninety-nine dollars and I've got two thousand and five hundred dollars. Well, let's see if I can make a deal like Dad does.*

I crawled out and looked at the owner saying, "There's a seep on the clutch housing. I'll be taking it back to Alaska on the Al-Can; sure wouldn't want to lose the clutch in the middle of winter in the Yukon Territory."

"Hey, it's been like that for years. They all start losing a little lube there," he answered.

"Maybe. Tell you what, how would you feel about twenty-five-hundred cash?"

"Deal," he said, sticking his hand out. We shook, and I explained I'd run to the bank and be back in an hour or so. Drove Mom's Pacer to Grandmother's, picked up the check and signed the promissory note. Drove to the bank and cashed her check, caught Clint coming home from high school and loaded him into the Pacer. I went back across town and delivered the money. We signed and countersigned the title, Clint took Mom's car home, and I drove my new-used L.C. home, picked up Mom at school and gave her the news.

"You didn't wait for your father to look at it!" Mom said.

"Mom, Dad has already taught me everything he knows about Land Cruisers, and I have managed to learn a few new things in Alaska."

"You should have waited. He'll be very angry."

Fortunately, it was a short trip home. I changed into my best shirt and slacks and slipped out to the new L.C. *Dad will hit the roof. Sure hope nothing goes wrong with it. Hmm, car needs a name.* I pondered a name, the path as a married man, and a bunch of other stuff. My proposal was already carefully rehearsed, but as I pulled up to Marsha's house, I ran through it one last time.

Marsha was dressed to kill: tight red sweater, short black skirt, and those legs—could look at those legs all day—she finished the whole thing with a pair of shiny black shoes.

After I told her where we were going, she must have guessed what's up. Oh well, hope she's not disappointed there isn't a ring, but I didn't know what size. We kissed hello, and I asked how her day was.

"More of the same. I'm having trouble, but I will finish this certification."

"Never doubted that, but just ask if I can help. I have a surprise for you."

"Really?" she asked innocently.

"Yeah, I bought a new-used Land Cruiser, right there," I said pointing to the beast parked at the curb.

"Wow, that's not what I expected," she said as we walked to the car.

"Yep, even got the guy to knock off six-hundred dollars." We had arrived at the passenger door, which I opened and held for her. She raised a foot to the running board, as I admired nearly the full length of her legs as her skirt rode up while she tried to step in and almost fell backwards.

"You'll need to grab the chicken bar," I directed.

"Huh, chicken bar?"

"Yeah, that handle over the glove compartment."

She leaned into the door and put both hands on the chicken bar, raised her right leg to the running board, and with a little assistance from me lifting her at the waist, she ended up facing the passenger seat. "Now what?"

"Turn around and sit." But she was already shuffling her feet around and then sat down.

I walked around to the driver's side and as I got in, she asked, "Why do you call it a chicken bar?"

"It's called a chicken bar because when you're off road sometimes, when it gets rough, a passenger will grab it to hang on. Then we call them chicken or a sissy. I think it's really called a 'passenger assist bar.' I need it sometimes when I'm getting out of the back seat," I explained. She slid as close as she could get on the 40/60 front seat. The driver has a bucket seat, 40%, and the passenger has 60% that in a pinch holds two people, depending on bottom size.

"It's not very nice to call people 'chicken' just because they're short," my five-foot two cutie told me. Then she asked, "Why do you keep changing the gear shift?"

"Because this really is a stick shift, unlike on automatics."

"I've seen stick shifts on the floor, but never on the steering wheel!" she told me.

Stop stupid, don't tell her it's the column, not the steering wheel. "It's actually a pretty common standard transmission, in this case 'three on the column'. I've also seen them with four or five gears."

"How does it work?"

"I'll teach you soon in an empty parking lot. It's called a 'H-pattern' because it makes a 'H' as you shift. Here, I'll show you." I came to a stop at a handy red light. "Okay, clutch in, brake on, lift the shifter up out of third and pull it back till it stops, push it down into first gear. If this was driver's ed, I would leave it in neutral, that's safer if your foot slips off the clutch, but most people leave it in first with the clutch in; lets you start faster. Green light, release the brake and at the same time release the clutch and give it some gas. Get rolling, foot off the gas, clutch in and shift into second, add gas as you let the clutch out. You don't need to leave it in second very long, then repeat the process and you're in third," I completed my lesson on using the 'H-pattern'.

Marsha said, "I'll never remember that. I learn by doing."

"Everyone has to, because every clutch engages differently, even in the same kind of cars."

"Don't you want an automatic?" Marsha asked.

"Nah, stick shift is much more useful. In fact, this lever on the dash if you pull it down puts the car into super low, you still have three speeds, but a lot more power for driving in mud or pulling stuff."

"Oh, Mom's out with her liquor salesman again. He wants to meet you. He brought a bottle, it's a beer. I've seen them. We need to plan dinner with him."

Marsha continued all the way to the restaurant. My only contribution was an occasional 'yes' or 'really'. I had already learned that she tended to talk pretty much nonstop unless she was mad, she avoided proper nouns, and you had to pay attention because you never knew when she would stop because she really wanted an answer. Usually if I was paying attention, I knew the understood subject. I would later find out that her brothers called it speaking Martian.

At the restaurant, we had a nice steak supper with champagne. Marsha didn't normally drink, but she liked champagne. She was also wild about baked potatoes. She ate most of mine since I was getting tired of potatoes except French fries. Our (her) conversation continued through supper as she paused to eat a bite of the tiramisu, forgetting my rehearsed proposal, I just blurted out, "Will you marry me?"

"Yes, let's not tell anyone for a while."

"Huh, I want to shout it to the world and take you to get a ring tomorrow!" *Wait, that's not the answer I expected.*

"I just think it's kind of soon. Everyone will ask how long we've been dating, saying that's not long enough. Should we waste money on a ring? They'll say I'm pregnant. Let's wait until we've lived together awhile, you might not be able to stand me."

The rambling barrage of objections floored me. Live together! Which do I answer first? "Don't you love me?" I set my champagne glass down. I was hurt and it showed in my voice.

She reached across and took my hands. "Yes, I love you. I just don't think we should announce our engagement yet." Her big brown eyes looked through me and oddly settled my fears.

"Okay, I guess I see what you mean." *Not really, this is going to require some thought.* "I've never told anyone I was going steady with a girl before. Can we start there?"

"Of course. We'll get married, but let's take it step by step," she answered.

The next morning, I announced that I was going steady with Marsha. Mom said, "We haven't even met this girl!" Dad grilled me with questions about her and her family. They finally settled on taking us both to supper that night. Marsha and I had an unplanned date already agreed upon. She said yes, she wanted to meet them.

We met Mom, Dad, and my brother Clint at a nice place downtown. The memory is a little vague. Marsha was wearing a short tight skirt because our table was at the back and we followed the hostess single file, Marsha and I bringing up the rear. I started following her with my eyes glued lustfully to her bottom and legs. Then I noticed an old man staring, which caused me to see the middle-aged man opposite him swiveling his head to watch. Then I noticed that practically every male close enough to see her from eight to eighty was staring. *Yeah, she's something, you horny devils, and she's mine, eat your heart out. Actually, you're hers.*

I had warned Marsha we Francisco's were big teasers, which she knew since my teases often confused her. She held her own through Dad's questions, jibes, and jabs. At one point, as my eyes lingered on our attractive waitress, Dad said, "Son, you're going steady now. You need to keep your eyes on Marsha."

Before I could answer, Marsha popped in with, "Just because he's on a diet doesn't mean he can't read the menu."

Dad laughed, saying, "Son, this one is a keeper."

Mom didn't look so sure.

Our courtship continued. I was also planning my drive back for the spring and final semester before graduation. Marsha was looking at maps with me when she said, "San Francisco isn't far out of your way. You'll be leaving soon enough that I could visit my brother and fly home. We'd get to spend more time together." Sounded like a good idea to me, so I contacted some friends in my dorm who were on the west coast for Christmas. Max and his brother, Eric, thought it would be fun and cheaper than flying. A friend of my father's son was planning to go to the electronics school at Anchorage Community College. Drake thought riding with me to Fairbanks, then taking the train to Anchorage was an adventure he wanted to be in on.

CHAPTER NINE

❦

NORTH TO ALASKA

Marsha, Drake, and I got Critter. Marsha felt bad the L.C. didn't have a name, so she christened it Critter with a bottle of beer. We said our goodbyes and, with me driving, Marsha sitting in the center and Drake on the right-side, we headed west on Interstate 80. Not sure if our parents expected Drake and I to share a room while Marsha slept in a single, but that alternative never came up.

Marsha and I decided not to register as husband and wife, but to be honest and tell motel clerks we were engaged. There was no problem the first night, but a snowstorm was slowing us down and at our overnight in Wyoming or Utah, the clerk asked to see Marsha's ID then excused herself.

Marsha looked at me, saying, "She's sure taking a long time. I would have caught hell if I had taken this long to check someone in." She had briefly been a night clerk at a downtown hotel before returning to college.

"Yeah, maybe she just needed the bathroom and couldn't wait."

We both began exploring the brochure rack. Shortly, a police officer arrived. The clerk came out to talk to the officer, who then politely introduced himself to us, then asked for our ID's.

Marsha told him we were engaged and on our way to her older brothers.

He examined the IDs, looked at the clerk, shrugging his shoulders, turned back to us saying, "Thank you for your cooperation.

Congratulations on your engagement. Have a good trip and drive safely." Then he was gone.

Marsha and I puzzled over what had happened into the night and again the next morning. I was going to ask the clerk, but a new one was on duty when I checked us out. The next day in Nevada, our motel had a mini-casino with slot machines off the office. I discovered that Marsha didn't share my boredom with slots, which surprised me since she usually was very frugal. As we played, the croupier came over and nicely asked Marsha for her ID. She demanded to know why. "Well, ma'am, you're very pretty and all, but you don't look eighteen."

Pulling her wallet out of her purse, she shoved her driver's license at him saying, "See, I'm twenty-one. You had better learn to judge people's age if you're going around checking IDs."

"I'm sorry, ma'am, but we could lose our license if we let underage people gamble, and we get a lot of high schoolers trying to slip by."

"I graduated from high school in 1969. I'm really tired of people who don't treat me like an adult."

Hanging his head and leaving, he said, "I'm sorry, but it's my job."

Marsha looked at me and said, "Let's get out of here. They don't deserve anymore of our money."

Best news I've had tonight. Much rather have you alone in the room, than here, pulling slot handles. "Let's go. Wow, you really tore that guy a new one. Why so angry? Most women like to be thought younger."

That was the wrong thing to say. She launched into an angry recitation of numerous incidents where she was treated like a child after her graduation. A clerk in a clothing store had told her, after a long frustrating search for a bra that fit right, "Don't worry honey, you'll fill out overnight anytime now." Marsha told her, "I'm twenty years old and I resent that comment. I'm reporting you." Which she did. She was still fuming over being fired from a department store when she had said something to a customer, who thought she had been called an old lady. Her tirade went on for a long time that night.

As I was dozing off, after she once again became her affectionate self, I had an insight. *The motel clerk must have called the police because she thought I was sexually molesting an underaged girl. Hmm, if people think she's so young, what must they think of me? Chester the molester?*

The next day, we drove out of the sunshine and into another snow storm. Weather allowing, the plan was to reach Marsha's brother's house in the Bay area. As we approached Donner Pass, the traffic on the left side increased. We soon discovered why: a large billboard designed to have messages hung on it declared the pass was closed to traffic unless they had four-wheel drive or chains. Trucks were pulled over on a pull-off, chaining up.

"Poor bustards, putting chains on in this kind of weather is the worst." The cars without the necessary equipment for the road ahead were turning back on a crossover built into the interstate for such eventualities.

"Do we need to turn back?" Marsha's voice seemed smaller than usual.

"Nope, we have the best four-wheel drive on the road, plus added four studded tires for Alaska. Tire guy was surprised at my order, but I already learned it's the best system for winter in Alaska."

Drake asked, "Any other Alaskan driving tips?"

"Err, probably you'll get filled in, but if you're buying a car or truck, studded tires on all four is a good idea. Just the drive wheels like many people do to save money doesn't work too well when you can't steer or stop. Four- wheel drive is nice, but if you stick to pavement, two- wheel drive will get you around. Oh, tires have a tendency to have a flat spot frozen into them when you're parked overnight. You start out the next day, the flat spot can break the seal and let all the air out of the tire—or tires. I went out on a couple of wrecker calls for people who had two to four flats. Nobody carries that many spares. The way to avoid the problem is to start off slow. More importantly, put tubes in your tubeless tires. Be sure they're natural rubber tubes; the synthetic ones seem to break into little pieces in the cold. Sure, they'll solve that one of these days. A lot of companies test parts in Fairbanks in the winter; if they'll work there, Iowa's no sweat."

We were crawling along in four high as we climbed the pass in the blizzard. In spite of my slow speed, I almost rear-ended a snowblower/

sander that was working on the road. Following him meant going even slower, but Marsha's gasps and cries of "Don't pass!" caused me to wisely relax and follow along. Often, the snowblower was obscured by swirling snow,but I always knew when I was getting close because of the sand hitting the windshield, often when the snowblower was still out of sight. I was unsuccessful in calming Marsha by reciting the history of the Donner Party. She hadn't heard it, leaving me once again wondering what they taught in parochial schools.

After a slow but safe crossing, we left the snowblower on the downhill and quickly began descending through the seasons, although the summer got lost somewhere as we went from spring to fall, though many people were dressed as if it were winter.

Traffic increased, and I began my graduate studies in driving. I dropped Drake at a friend's house and continued trying to drive like a Californian, reading a map and watching for turns. I discovered, sadly, map reading was not a skill Marsha had. We did finally discover Tom and Lana's home. Marsha was upstairs, I think in the children's room, but I never made it up the stairs. I had a piece of floor in the den, but my Thermorest and sleeping bag made it quite comfortable. I found I really missed Marsha.

During our short stay, Marsha and I toured the Bay area, doing all the tourist stops. She woke me up early before the rest of the house on my last day and gave me more than a kiss goodbye. After breakfast, I began driving around the Bay Area, picking up Drake, Max, and his brother Eric for the trip back to Fairbanks.

Driving in California and Oregon at that time was challenging due to the gasoline shortage. After driving across half the country and hearing about the gas crisis on the news and not encountering any difficulty buying gas, the higher prices didn't bother me since my years in Alaska had adjusted my mindset to high gas prices. Drake, Marsha, and I had concluded that the "gas shortage" was a way to increase the price without taking responsibility.

Then we got to California. We passed a few short lines at gas stations, but many stations had "Closed! Out of gas, try tomorrow!"

signs out. It was worse in northern California. We passed station after station that was closed.

As my quarter tank of gas approached fumes, I told the guys, "Looks like we'll have to stop at the first motel next to a gas station. I'll get in line and sleep in the car and come get you when I'm full. If this keeps up, it's going to be a long trip to Fairbanks."

As I began searching at a very fuel stretching speed, I saw an open station, made a right and pulled up to a pump. As the attendant came towards us, we climbed out to stretch and a big crew-cab pick-up rumbled in behind the Land Cruiser. This wasn't a clean, shiny, urban pickup, but a rough and tumble 4x4 that obviously worked for a living. The truck barely stopped, taking a threatening stance less than an inch from the L.C.'s rear bumper. With a roar of: "I'll kill you, that's my gas! You Goddamned tourist," a huge man, in classic lumberjack garb, plaid wool shirt and dirty Carhartt pants hit the ground from the driver's door of the pick-up and charged towards me.

During my stretch, I had noticed the police station across the street. I broke into a run for the front door. *Can I outrun this guy? He has an angle on me. Have to open the door when I get there. Will a cop be just inside?*

Unseen by me, the attendant, a small but brave teenager, broke into a run, getting between me and my would-be murderer, screaming, "I have enough gas for both of you."

I stopped in the middle of the street—luckily there was no traffic. My savior stood with the lumberjack towering over him. I could hear that they were talking, but couldn't make out the words though I saw the attendant point to the second pump. The lumberjack turned and headed back to his truck. I walked up behind the attendant saying, "Thank you, you saved my life."

"Yeah, people are getting crazy over gas. Fill you up?"

"Yes, but maybe do him first just in case."

"Naw, we have plenty," he said as we walked back to the El Coyote. We had to stop for the lumberjack's truck as he pulled around my car. I winced, expecting to hear our wing mirrors collide.

They didn't, but I was glad I couldn't see how close they were. With my help—L.C.'s have a very sharp turn in the filler tube that doesn't allow filling the tank on the high setting, at least until you have established a flow of gas—the attendant started filling my car. Then he headed for the monster's truck. As he filled it, the lumberjack and he conversed. We couldn't hear them until the lumberjack said loudly, for our benefit, "They shouldn't let tourists buy gas." Business done, we continued on to Oregon City and Scott's house.

CHAPTER TEN

FOLLOWED

We continued up the coast Highway 101 so we could enjoy the scenery you miss on the interstate. Highway 18 is a diagonal to the NE that we took for two reasons: to get to Scott's house in Oregon City and to pick up Inter state 5 to speed-up the journey. As enjoyable as the coast road was, it was slower than the interstate and we had a long way to go. Night fell, and I was driving a remote stretch with a wall of trees on each side, making it seem like we were in a black tunnel. The only light was the headlights lighting a small section of blacktopped highway.

Suddenly, there was a spot of light in the rearview mirror. It grew rapidly, too rapidly, quickly resolving itself into a pair of headlights on high beam, flooding the Land Cruiser with light, causing a blinding reflection in the mirror. I shouted, "Brace for impact!" as it became obvious the driver wasn't changing lanes to pass, and was coming way too fast to stop before hitting us.

Shoulder to narrow to escape right. Left lane is empty, what if he plans to swoop around us or a car comes from opposite direction? Too dark to see if there is a curve hiding oncoming traffic. Push the pedal to the metal!

Critter leaped forward. The headlights closed in. Someone said, "Relax, we won't get hurt as bad!" The others may have gone limp, but I was trying to push the accelerator through the floor and had a death grip on the steering wheel. The lights zoomed up behind us, but stayed just a foot or two from the rear bumpers.

No impact. Can't be hooked to us. Hugging Critter like a trailer. Wow, we are going way too fast to be this close together. Wonder what happens if I slow down?

I began gently easing up on the gas. As we slowed, the following car matched us exactly.

"Kim, what's this guy doing? Let him pass!"

"I'm trying, but the slower I go, the slower he goes. Wonder if he needs help?"

"More likely there's a bunch of them, and if we stop they jump out and kill us," someone said.

I continued slowing down and easing over onto what little shoulder there was. Our close companion held his position.

"There are two steel extension bars for the jack under the left back seat. Someone get them out. Give one to Max and be ready to hand one to me when I step out."

"What are you going to do?" asked Max as the crank handle touched his shoulder.

"Just pull over as far as I can and stop. Then get out and see what he wants. Just taking the crank handles in case there's a fight."

Critter slowly came to a stop with the right wheels on the edge of the pavement. I dropped out the driver's door, armed with the crank handle, but kept it to my side. As I stepped out of the glare of the headlights, I could see the driver's head was leaning against his steering wheel. "Looks like he's sick. I'm going to see if he needs help."

I opened the driver's side door of the sedan that was behind us. In the weak overhead light, I could see the driver motionless against the steering wheel. "Hey, do you need help?"

No response.

I shook his shoulder and repeated, "Can I help you?" Just like first aid class. No response. I conducted a quick visual inspection, but didn't see any blood and the pulse in his neck seemed good.

"What do you think?" Max asked from the dark at my shoulder.

I jumped, startled. The whole gang seemed to be there as I turned around. "Smells like a distillery. He's not dead, just dead drunk.

Probably best to just leave him and stop at the next phone and call troopers. Hope no one meaner than us finds him."

Someone asked, "Should we leave someone here?"

The group was already breaking for the car. A voice said, "Are you volunteering?"

"No, just wondering."

Feeling guilty, I headed down the road watching for any chance to use a phone and keeping track of miles traveled since leaving our drunk. Finally, really only eight or nine miles, as I recall, we hit a truck stop on the edge of the next town.

I stopped and filled up since they had gas. Everyone else broke for the rest rooms and junk food. While the car was filling, I called the local police and told them where to find the drunk. They said they would take care of it. Fresh coffee in hand, actually in the hands of the guy sitting next to me, we finished driving to Scott's, and spread our sleeping bags out on the family room floor.

CHAPTER ELEVEN

❧

ALASKA HIGHWAY

The trip north through Washington and British Columbia on Interstate 5 and BC 97 to Dawson Creek was uneventful, except it seemed to be snowing most of the time. Dawson Creek is the "official" start of the Alaska Highway. We continued north, on what was then, still, a gravel highway. It wasn't very pleasant in the summer, dusty and rough. Middle of winter was great. All the potholes were filled with packed snow and no dust. This allowed driving at speeds that pushed what was safe. The only problem was the truck traffic. Oncoming trucks created a blinding ground blizzard as they passed. Visibility became so bad that the driver—we were taking turns—sometimes had to coast to a stop until the snow settled.

Thirty miles or so out of Fort Nelson, where I had taken the wheel, on one of the many hairpin curves an oncoming semi was taking his half out of the middle. As I tried to hug the shoulder closely enough to make room for the road hog, the right front wheel got caught by the soft snow off the shoulder. Critter would have turned over if I tried to pull back on the road. I straightened the wheels, pulling straight into the ditch. It wasn't steep and the snow slowed Critter quickly, but gently.

All right. Good decision. Just stop and back out on the path I packed down. What the hell? Just as we were stopping, the L.C.'s left front tire climbed up into the air. In slow motion the left side came up, Critter hesitated, then fell over onto its right side. The car was filled with swear words, 'get off me', and 'what the hell.'

I shouted over the din, "Is anybody hurt?"

"Err, I'm okay."

"Fine here, but all this stuff back here is a mess."

"Okay here."

"Alright, I'll climb out the door and help the rest of you out. Then we'll figure out what to do," I said, unfastening my seat belt, which dropped me on Eric, who was sitting next to me, crushing poor Max against the right door, which had become the floor. There once again was a lot of swearing as the three of us in the front sorted ourselves out to the new relative position of the car. I got my feet into the narrow gap between the driver's seat and the 60% bench seat.

Standing up, I was able to get the driver's side door open and resting on my head. Pushing myself up, I was able to get both hands on the running board so I could lift and pull myself out of poor Critter. Once on top, I found a foothold on the exposed frame and held the door open with one hand while Eric climbed out, followed by Max and finally Drake.

Out on the ground, we got our boots tied, coats zipped, and I stomped through the snow at the front of the car. "Shit, a stump!" I kicked the snow away from the tree stump that the left front tire climbed, tipping us over. "Damn it, I thought we made it. Would have made it except for this stump." I stamped around the car, inspecting for damage and looking for more stumps. Finally, the physical exertion controlling my anger, I said. "Look at that. One damn stump under the snow and I hit. What luck!"

"Yeah, I thought you had it made, we almost stopped. At least you didn't have a head-on with the semi," Max was always good for finding the bright spot.

"The car looks alright," Drake said from the roof side.

"Do you think we can turn it over?"

"We can try. Should be able to back right out if we can. Let's all join Drake," I suggested.

Everyone found a hand hold, squatted in the snow, and heaved.

"It moved a little, let's go again on three," someone said. I didn't think it had, but repositioned myself and gave it my best on three. Nothing.

Someone said, "I could move the world with a lever if I had a place to stand."

"Fan out and see if you can find any levers," I suggested.

We walked into the woods on four different paths. We found several downed trees we could drag back. Testing revealed only two that didn't break easily, but we decided that would be enough and fit them under the front and rear bumpers. With a strong enough lever, we might have flipped the car, but both of ours broke. My lungs burned from sucking in cold air as my exertions had caused me to breath heavily, filling the air with my frozen exhales. Everyone else's heads were also surrounded by frozen breaths.

Through the icy stillness, Eric heard a truck. His announcement was greeted with derision. He angrily said, "Listen!" We did, and now, we could hear it too. We hurried up to the highway, arriving just as the truck rounded the bend heading south.

We all managed to find the energy to do jumping jacks, which had the desired effect as the truck used its engine brake, further distributing the cold still air. You can't stop that much momentum quickly, particularly on a snow- covered road. We all headed for the stopped truck where it rested down the road.

"Some of you wait here! He'll think he's being hijacked." With no discussion, the others slowed to a walk, leaving me to get to the truck and climb-up on the running board. A blast of warm air struck my face as the driver lowered the window about a third of the way.

"Looks like you had an accident," he said.

Brilliant! Kim be nice, don't mention why. You need a friend to help. "Yeah, I got too close to the shoulder and sucked in. Tree stump in the ditch flipped me over."

"Climb in, I'll take you to Fort Nelson. You can get a tow truck there."

"Err, okay, but I'm pretty sure I can back out if you have a chain; we can flip it back on its wheels," I suggested.

"Nope, I can take you to Fort Nelson."

"Okay, thank you. I'll tell my buddies and hop in.

"Okay, don't be long."

I stepped off the running board as he closed the window, turning to the guys, who were collected at the back of the trailer. I said, "I'm off to Fort Nelson. Build a fire. I'll be back with a tow truck. If someone flips the car over, back out and wait here. Might miss each other if you follow us."

I walked around and climbed into the cab. It was hot. The driver was in a light shirt. *No wonder he didn't want to flip us. Nice and warm in here. I suppose time is money for these guys.*

As I introduced myself, he put the truck in gear and headed down the highway. Other than it being very hot, I don't remember much about the trip back to FT. Nelson. The service station where I had filled up on my way north had an assortment of cars and trucks parked about and a hand painted sign saying towing at the bottom of a list of services available under big capital letters: LAST CHANCE FOR GAS. The driver dropped me off and I waited in the office for the attendant to have a free moment. He finished filling my ride and came into the office asking, "What'd you need?"

"My Land Cruiser is flipped on its side in the ditch up the road about thirty miles. I could use a tow truck."

"Well, I have one, but I have to call and get a driver. I'm here alone."

"Okay, don't suppose you trust me with the tow truck?" I asked.

"Sorry, don't know you kid."

I sat in a wobbly chair in the corner and he made some calls between filling cars and trucks. Finally turned to me smiling, "Got a guy to come in. but he'll be an hour or so."

Two hours later, we were in the tow truck's cab headed north to Critter, which I hoped the guys hadn't burned to stay warm. I don't remember much of my conversation with the driver except I had to assure him I would do any crawling in the snow needed to right the Land Cruiser.

We arrived and the guys had a nice fire going in the ditch downwind of Critter. The driver released the tow cable. Grabbing the hook, I walked down to the L.C. and the gang. "Good thinking, building the fire downwind of the car. Less chance of burning Critter," I greeted them.

"What took you so long?" they asked.

"Long story, let's save it for the road. Hmm, the question now is how do we hook the cable on to flip the thing?" I had pulled a lot of cars and trucks out of snow filled ditches working for College Auto, but none had ever been on their side. We combined all of our knowledge in a discussion with four different ideas. The driver called from the road, "Hey, I gotta get back, hook it up."

"Alright, it's my car, we'll try my way first." I passed the hook through the left hook shaped rear bumper (top of car laying on its side). "Take it away," I said to the driver.

He engaged the winch, the cable tightened, and Critter began sliding through the tracks it had left coming down into the ditch. Critter caught on something. I almost hollered stop, but noticed the resistance was causing the right side to lift off the snow. "Grab the high side. Pull it down. Stay clear of cable. Watch out for car flipping."

A lot was happening fast and I had visions of my friends being cut in half by a snapping cable or crushed under a car flipping over. Two guys were under the right side, first lifting then pushing. I was pulling the left front wheel and a fourth was pulling down on the left running board. What started slowly ended suddenly as the car passed its balance point, falling onto its wheels with crash. I barely backed up in time to avoid the tire crushing my feet. Jim was in the snow on his back legs, escaping injury by sliding under the L.C.

I hollered at him, "You okay?" Seeing the car rolling backwards now, I added "GET OUT OF THERE! STOP THE WINCH!"

The driver stopped the winch, Jim was backstroking through the snow out from under the car. The driver shouted, "It was coming. Why did you stop me?"

"I want to center the cable so the car doesn't flip again," I replied. *Guess he didn't see the danger.*

"Wow, that was neat," came from the right side of the car. Jim was on his feet, brushing off snow. Relieved, I walked to the left rear hook bumper, asking the driver, "Little slack, please."

He took the winch out of gear and the cable sagged. I gave it a tug and got enough slack to take the hook off the left bumper. I pulled out some more cable as I walked to the center of the tailgate. Briefly thought about hooking it to the spare tire mount, but knowing better, I dropped to my knees in the snow, then onto my belly, pushing through to a crossbeam in the frame. I fumbled with the hook a few times. *Need to be able to feel my hands to do this. Damn gloves aren't helping at all.*

Mission accomplished, I crawled out and told the driver, "Take it away." *Far away. What kind of lunatic drives this damn highway in the middle of winter?* Critter followed the cable obediently through the snow, up the shoulder, which was more snow berm that the plows had left than road shoulder, and finally onto the highway again.

I unhooked Critter, letting the tow-driver worry about his loose cable. I jumped into the driver's seat, inserting the key and with a prayer, turned the key. The engine turned over, *good,* but I continued to crank, *one Mississippi, two Mississippi eighteen give up at twenty,* cough, splutter, *vroom.* "GREAT! Good old Critter still runs." I pushed in the choke slowly and she settled into a steady idle.

The guys had opened the back and were reloading our stuff as they brought it up out of the ditch. Tipping over had made a jumble out of it, so they had unloaded while waiting for me to return with the tow truck. I took time to take an appraising look at Critter. The obvious damage was to the windshield. Interestingly, the safety glass was intact, but the right of the corner of the frame was bent. This had caused a gap between the top of the frame and roof at the right corner. The bending of the frame had also caused the glass to pop out of the frame so the center was still in, but there were gaps several inches wide on each side.

Doesn't look too serious. Glass shop can probably pop the window back in. As brittle as glass gets in this subzero air, I better not try here. Need a heated garage. Kim, the engine!

I jumped out of the car and onto the ground on my back, sliding under Critter. *Nothing dripping off into the snow. Check skid plate.* Past experience had taught me leaks had a way of collecting in the skid plate and not being visible on the ground. Taking my right glove off, I reached up at the back of the plate where there was a gap and felt around. Hard to tell cold from wet by feel, but a visual inspection of my hand just found greasy dirt. Crawling out, I opened the hood, looking in at the engine.

"Everything looks good."

Startled, I jumped and looked at the tow driver, the source of my surprise.

"Yeah, looks like I got off lucky. Can you guys fix that windshield?"

He looked, checking both sides, and came back.

"I'm pretty sure we can't get the glass out without breaking it. Then we would have to order a new one and straighten the frame. You're talking a week or two. You'd be better off getting to a shop where you live."

"Okay. Thanks. Going to be cold driving like this to Fairbanks."

"Yeah, glad it's you, not me. What with the deposit, why don't we call it good? I want to get home."

"Okay, thanks." He left.

We put on all the clothes we had and headed out into the gloomy evening.

The rest of the trip was *cold!* We all ended up in our sleeping bags which seemed to keep us from getting hypothermia. Everyone had their bags pulled up and over their head, that is but the driver. We resisted temptation to cut eye, arm, and leg holes in a sleeping bag so the driver could also be completely covered. My bag was a large rectangular model, so the driver used it, with the draw string pulled tight under the arms, the open "back" (the side normally) against the seat. Since it was completely unzipped, the driver's feet were free to operate the gas, brake, and clutch. Hands were still a problem. We had consolidated all of our gloves and mittens to come up with a set of tight-fitting gloves next to the skin, thick gloves for extra insulation and a large pair of mittens that went over them all. The driver's hands still got cold, shifts at the wheel were reduced to about an hour.

I don't think we missed anything that was open. Most service stations and restaurants were seasonal in those days, only remaining open in the tourist season (summer for non-Alaskans). Whitehorse was a blessing since Max and I had a friend there.

Don't remember if he had planned to join us for the trip to Fairbanks or not, but he wisely chose not to after seeing four frozen people at his door. It was so wonderful to be warm again. There was talk of continuing by bus at least among my passengers. I decided I wouldn't leave Critter in Whitehorse for repair, but instead would tough it out to Fairbanks, where I was sure my friend, Mike Wheat, could help me do the repairs on the cheap. To my surprise, no one jumped ship, but decided to continue to share my suffering which did make it less.

When we crossed the Canada-US border, at Beaver Creek, it was-70 F on the border station's thermometer. We were all inside before the border guard could finish getting into his parka. The two guys on duty were kind to us and let us warm up and drink their hot coffee. I don't remember if they inspected us.

We followed the rolling Richardson Highway. It had lots of permafrost heaves in those days hence the name: rolling. Arrived at Lathrop Hall at the University of Alaska. Max and Eric already had their keys from fall semester. I think I took Drake to the Alaska Railroad because he was continuing his education at University of Alaska Anchorage (I think it was Anchorage Community College then) I settled in for my final semester.

CHAPTER TWELVE

WE WON'T
REGISTER YOU

"The Cremation of Sam Magee" took on new meaning for the four us. I stood under a hot shower for a long time. Every time I stepped out, a chilly draft would drive me back in. Finally, looking like a boiled lobster, I crawled into bed.

A few days later was registration. Once again dressed warmly, my checkbook in my hip pocket and a file full of registration papers in my gloved hand, I headed across campus to the Bunnel Building. The line almost stretched outside. I made it through the outer doors into the arctic entryway where I waited and chatted until the line advanced into the hallway. We slowly but surely advanced down a long hallway towards the registrar's office. The office door was flanked by two desks where two students hired for the rush checked the registration papers, and took the money for classes, dorm rent, and meal tickets if you were living on campus. I noticed a young woman, whom I had given a ride home to after a graduation party last spring, was sitting at one of the desks. I figured parting with most of my money to a friendly face would be easier than to a stranger. I juggled my position in line so I would register with Carol.

"Hi, Kim. How was your break?"

Handing her my file, I said, "Great. I got engaged and had a wonderful boat trip down the Yukon River." I fancied I saw a flash of disappointment at my news, but it was probably my imagination. "How's everything going for you and your son?"

"Good. I'm full time now in the registrar's office, but they let me take my classes so I should graduate this spring. Hope they'll let me continue on after graduation." She was multitasking as we talked, scanning my paperwork. "Kim, this won't work. Scientific Sampling and Vertebrate Biology are at the same time on Monday, Wednesday, Friday."

"Yeah, I need them both to graduate and they both are only offered in the spring semester. I'll get lecture notes from another student when I miss class."

"Sorry, I can't register you with the conflict. You're going to have to get written permission from both professors and your advisor."

"Bummer, can't get you to let it slip through?" I asked.

"No, I need this job and the details are important."

Smiling, I said, "Okay. Guess I have some professors to find." She handed me the file and I headed out the door with the registered but poorer students.

My student advisor, Dr. Dean, was in and I explained my problem. He scribbled a note to the registrar saying, "Guess we should have done all these permissions when we set up this schedule last fall. Good to see you back. Did you have a good break?"

"Yeah, great. Got to float the Yukon from Tanana to the mouth. Shot a load of pheasants and got engaged."

"Congratulations, sounds like you had a busy break. Better let you go so you can get permission slips from the two professors."

"Thanks, I'm off."

I walked back to the door of the building, stopping once again to zip up my coat, pull down my stocking cap, pull up my hood and pull on my gloves. *Man, this going in and out is a pain. Must be a better way.*

I crossed the center of the campus, pausing briefly to look at the igloo the engineering students had built. *Wonder if they know that's culturally inappropriate. None of the Alaska natives used snow igloos.*

The Scientific Sampling professor was swamped with students, phone calls, and paperwork. His secretary quickly typed up a note to the registrar, signed it with her initials, and I was off to find Dr. Morrow:

the Vertebrate Biology professors and head of the Fisheries school. His secretary listened to my sad tale, but said she needed Dr. Morrow's permission to write me a note. She buzzed through on the intercom and asked if he had time to see me. "No, make an appointment."

She looked up at me, as I said, "Hey, registration is today, late fees start tomorrow. When should I come back today?" I emphasized today.

She looked down at his date book, looked back at my desperate expression, and rang through on the intercom again.

"Dr. Morrow, you don't have a free appointment for two weeks and this is a registration problem. I'm sorry, but it has to be dealt with today," she said very humbly.

He growled back. "Send him in."

He was glaring at his door as I opened it, "Make it fast."

"Yes, sir. Your class and Scientific Sampling are at the same time. I have my advisor's and the Scientific Sampling professor's permission to take both classes, but I need yours or they won't let me finish registering," I replied.

"How will you pass my course if you don't attend class?"

"I'll borrow lecture notes from another student and attend on test days. It will be hard, but I'm confident I can do it," I said.

"So, you're already planning to skip my lectures?"

"Yes, sir. I'm sure I'll miss them. I enjoy biology much more than math, but math is harder for me, so I'm trying to be realistic about where I'll need to spend the most time," I explained. *Don't tell him his former students warned you that his lectures are a bore and just a repetition of the text.*

"You can't pass my course without attending class," he said with great emphasis.

Now what do I say? Time to speak, Kim.

"I have a 4.0 average in biology classes. I have to have Vertebrate Biology to graduate this spring. I don't want to wait until next spring when it is offered next to take a single 200 level course." *Oops maybe shouldn't have mentioned it's a sophomore course. Beg.* "Please, sir, let me try. If I can't handle it, I will drop one of the courses and finish next spring."

Dr. Morrow thought for a moment. "Alright, but you will fail." He pushed the intercom button on his desk phone and told his secretary, "Type up a permission slip. Who am I to stand in the way of failure?"

Should I ask if he's going to give me a chance, or have I already failed? Nah, better just see what happens. "Thank you." I stepped back out to the secretary who was done typing and was stamping his name on the signature line. She handed me the note saying, "I never thought he would give you permission. Be ready to work hard."

"I will. Looks like I'm in for a tough semester. Thanks. Bye." Back to the registration line and waiting. I finally reached Carol again.

"Kim, go on in. We aren't supposed to register you. You really pissed the registrar off."

"Thanks for the head's up. Here goes." I stepped into the registrar's waiting area and up to her private office door. My knock was answered by, "Come in, if it's important."

I guess it's important. To me anyway. Think I've made more enemies today that in my whole life.

Stepping into her office, she looked up from the computer run she was working on. "Hmph, take a seat." She returned to work. She finished scanning the run, making some corrections. When she reached the bottom of the page she folded the page over at the perforation to the next page. Then she looked up at me over the top of her half lens reading glasses. "Well, have you fixed your schedule?"

"No." Her eyes flashed as anger filled her expression. "But I have notes from my advisor and both professors saying I can take the classes together. As required by the rules." I handed her the three permission slips.

She waved them away, glaring at me. "You are not taking two classes at once!

Control yourself. Getting angry won't help. I've taken enough shit today! I'm letting her have it. Control yourself. With clenched teeth, I counted the paperwork out of my file onto her desk. "Here's last fall's preregistration. Here's the notes from each professor and my advisor. Here's the check for my tuition, dorm fees, and meal ticket. If you won't accept them,

I won't leave this chair until you give me a dated receipt saying you refused to accept them." My jaws ached as we continued our stare down.

She blinked first. "Here." And she scrawled: "Refused to register due to class conflict." She stamped it with her date stamp and signed on the front of my registration.

"Thank you," I said through clenched teeth as I gathered all my paperwork into the file folder which I picked up as I left the room.

Later that evening, I ran into Carol as my friends and I were headed to the Khyber Inn in Wood's Hole. The student center at U of A, over the objections of the student government, it had been named by the president William Randolph Wood "The William Randolph Wood Student Center." The student body immediately renamed it Wood's Hole..

"Kim, what are you going to do about graduating since you're not registered?"

"I have my room in the dorm, my class schedule, and a kitchen in the dorm. So I plan to carry on as normal until someone wants to see my paperwork. Then I think your boss will be in trouble, not me."

Shaking her head no, she said, "I don't know if that will work. Good luck."

"Thanks, I'll probably need it." Then we parted ways. As I watched her pretty body going out the door, I thought, *If not for Marsha, I wonder if it would have worked out between us? Kim, Marsha's perfect, don't think such thoughts.*

CHAPTER THIRTEEN

MARSHA'S NORTH TO ALASKA

March 9th, and it had been below zero for a week or more. Fairbanks was thick with ice fog caused by the inversion trapping the air, while furnaces and vehicle exhaust filled the air with ice crystals. I had plugged Critter in to warm the engine twelve hours before I needed to go to the airport and pick up Marsha. Now I was waiting impatiently, walking back and forth in front of the window in the Pan Am waiting area trying to wish the arrival of the Boeing 707.

They announced the arrival of the flight and I scrambled to be first in the line of greeters waiting at the left side of the door from the ramp.

Then up the stairs came Marsha's beautiful face, red nosed from the short trip across the taxiway from the plane to stairway in the airport. Her dark blonde hair (often less flatteringly described as dishwater blonde) spilled over the collar of her new green down jacket. As she stepped off the plane, she was looking for me out in the terminal, and was startled when I scooped her into my arms.

"Cutie, it's been too long."

"Kim! You surprised me," she said, startled. I bent to kiss her and she gave me a quick peck, whispering, "Not here, later."

"Okay, let's go get your luggage." I took her carry-on, put my arm around her waist, and led her out of the crowd towards the escalator to baggage claim.

She began asking about how cold it was, how I was, and how Critter was in her usual rapid-fire manner, never waiting for a complete answer. We hit an open area outside of the departing and arriving passengers and their supporters. I stopped and bent down again, dropping her carry-on, and taking her in my arms. This time she returned the kiss and we stood locked in an embrace until we needed to breathe.

We reorganized and headed once again for the escalator. She leaned her head into my arm saying, "I'm sorry I didn't write more. All those letters and poetry…I really should have answered better."

"It's okay. You warned me you weren't a writer many times."

"I loved your letters," she said.

"I was afraid you wouldn't come after my terrible poetry."

"I thought they were sweet, feel like I know everyone already," she said as we arrived at the luggage carousel.

"It usually takes ten to twenty minutes for the bags to start. Let's go to this side, people all stand shoulder to shoulder three deep there where the bags first come out. You might find Alaskan luggage is a little different than what you've seen before," I warned. "You'll need to get a hat on. Critter has a few extra leaks since Wheat's friend, Wheat, and I fixed the windshield frame and roof."

"Yeah, you wrote about that, but I didn't understand. I don't understand this Wheat guy, sounds terrible and then nice, what is he?"

"He's D. Mikael Wheat. A great friend, but he's lewd and crude, though I guess most of us are like that," I replied, unable to really describe my unique friend's character.

"What's this titty twister habit of his?"

"Oh, probably shouldn't have mentioned that, but thought you should be ready in case my warning to him to keep his hands off didn't work. He's so bold and confident that he's always grabbing women by the breast with his thumb and forefinger shouting, 'Titty twister!' Which of course results in cries of pain, slaps, and sometimes tears. One girl didn't react and now the poor thing is labeled 'falsie'."

"He better keep his hands to himself with me," Marsha hissed, using a facial expression I hadn't seen before.

Wow, don't want to be on the receiving end of that expression. "He usually leaves girlfriends and wives alone," I said, hoping it would never become an issue.

"Is it going to be okay for me to stay in the dorm?" Marsha asked.

"No problem. The RA and her husband already know,

I think we'll be the third couple on the floor. I think the one girlfriend is just there a lot, I think she still has a dorm room in another dorm."

"Yeah, but I'm not a student," she continued.

"Not a problem, I don't think Wheat's girlfriend is a student either."

"How does that guy have a girlfriend?" a surprised Marsha asked.

"Hey, there's someone for everyone, even me," I said, pulling her close.

"There's nothing wrong with you," she said, giving me a peck. "I tried bad boys, but you're a lot easier to love."

Easier to love? Hmm, didn't really feel like I had a choice. Women must fall in love differently than men. Must talk to Marsha about that sometime. "Here comes the luggage, I'll bet Alaskan luggage will be different than what you're used to." To prove my point, an airplane propeller was the second piece to come out.

"Is that a propeller?"

"Yeah, they allow three pieces so if you only have one bag you can bring other stuff." About then, a waxed cardboard salmon box came out wrapped in fiber tape.

"Is that frozen fish?" she asked.

"It's the kind of box that frozen salmon are packed in to be shipped, but that box looks well-worn so I'm sure someone is using it as a trunk for stuff someone bought in Anchorage. The boxes are tough and waterproof, so they get reused all the time." Army surplus duffle bags, cardboard boxes, trunks, backpacks and even some suitcases came out.

Marsha's big Samsonite suitcase she had borrowed from her mothe and Marsha's smaller soft sided suitcase came out. Unlike the Alaskan who had boarded in Seattle and Anchorage, Marsha only had tw pieces since that was the limit on the United Air flight she had taken from Des Moines to Seattle. Alaskans got special treatment; the airline allowed three pieces of luggage instead of two before applying exces baggage charges.

I picked up her bags and led the way to the outside doors. The glas was opaque with thick frost. "Cutie, you felt the cold coming in from the plane, but it's a lot further to Critter. Even on full blast, you'll barel notice the heater. So let's get you bundled up. Where's your hat?"

"I don't need a hat."

"Yes, you do. Remember what the old sourdough said to th Cheechoo: 'if your feet are cold put your hat on,'" I quoted to her.

"My feet aren't cold!" she said, puzzled.

"They will be if you don't put your hat on."

"Okay." She produced a knit beret from her coat pocket. Setting i jauntily on her head. "There!" she said emphatically.

"Cute as hell, but your ears will get cold. Too late to buy a stockin hat now, guess that will have to do since there's not a hood on your coat If you get cold, I'll put my hood up and let you have my hat."

"I don't want to wear that."

"You will when your ears get cold. Your gloves are too thin, but yo can put your hands in your pocket. Let's go," I said, picking up her gea and holding the door open with my back. She stepped past me and followed her out into the below-zero night.

She had tiny low-cut shoes, so I had to put everything down and lif her over the snow berm and into the parking lot. By the time we reache the car, she had shrunk with her head huddled into her shoulders an her hand buried deep in her pockets. I opened Critter's door and lifte her onto the running board so she could get in.

"I'm cold."

"I told you. Do you want my hat?"

"No, I want you to close the door and start the car."

Won't help, even with the radiator blocked, it takes forever for the engine to get hot enough to put out any heat, but what the hell.

Closing the door, I left her stuff on the pavement and went around to the driver's side and fired up the engine. She already knew how the heater worked so she turned it on high.

Still doesn't believe me that it's an extension of the radiator and high just slows down engine warming up and heat to the cab. Oh well, she'll get it after a few cold trips. I moved the luggage around to the rear, unhooking the spare and opening bottom tailgate so I could slide it in. Opening the top half would have really flooded the L.C. with cold air. All buttoned up, I climbed into Critter next and even smaller Marsha with her legs tucked under her on the seat. I put my arm around her shoulders saying, "I'll warm you up when we get back to the dorm."

"Does Critter ever get warm?"

"Not in the winter. That's why we need to take you shopping tomorrow.

"Good."

We drove off taking Airport Road to the University. Marsha sprinted for the dorm door while I plugged Critter's engine heater into the socket at my parking spot and unloaded her gear. Then I followed her in and led the way to my room on the second floor.

CHAPTER FOURTEEN

YOU'RE NOT REGISTERED

As Earth Sciences and Human Affairs (a freshman course required for my degree that almost slipped under the radar) was dismissed, the instructor asked me to come up before I left. *Geez, I can't help it, this course is a drag. Guess I'll have to put out some more effort.*

Instead of the lecture on not working up to my potential he simply handed me a note. I followed my classmates out into the hall, stopped and leaned against the wall to read the note.

They finally noticed. Well, off to my room to get my file, then time to play the bureaucratic game.

"Hi, I'm Richard Kim Francisco, call me Kim, I have a note to report here." I slid the note across the reception station to a woman I recognized from seeing her on campus.

Come to the registrar's office immediately.

"Just a moment." She checked some notes on a pad, then placed an interoffice phone call.

Shortly, the registrar came out of her office, spoiling for a fight judging by her facial expression.

Oh shit! Stay calm. You're in the right here.

"Young man, you may not go to this university without enrolling and paying your fees."

"If you recall, I offered to pay my fees, but you refused to take them. Here's a copy of your receipt," I answered, struggling to maintain a civil tone.

"That doesn't mean anything. You owe a hundred dollars in tuition and one-thousand-five hundred and forty-five dollars in late fees. You need to pay for your dorm and meal ticket, or we'll have you arrested for trespass."

Stay calm. She's losing it. That "worthless" receipt is troubling her.

"I will pay what I owed when you refused to register me. Not one penny in late fees. My late registration is your fault, not mine. Please call the police and try to arrest me for trespass. I'll call the public defender's office and the News Miner (Fairbanks' newspaper)."

The small group of her employees that were watching from a safe distance seemed to enjoy her reaction. She was at a loss for words and turned very red in the face. Then she exploded. "YOU WILL PAY LATE FEES! I'LL SEE TO IT!" before she stormed off into her office.

The receptionist said quietly, "I think she's calling the police? She's calling someone." She pointed to the five buttons across the bottom of her phone; one was lit up.

"Would you be so kind as to call Harris Shelton's office for me?"

"What would I tell him?"

"Nothing, I just prefer to use your phone rather than give the appearance I escaped."

"Oh sure." She checked the intercampus phone sheet, dialed a couple of numbers, and handed me the receiver.

I caught Carol's eye as she shook with suppressed laughter. When our eyes met, she shook her head negatively.

"Dean Sheldon's office. How may I help you?"

"Hi. This is Richard Kim Francisco. I'm down in the registrar's office and I think I'm about to be arrested. The student handbook says Dr. Sheldon is the first person to call if you are arrested or going to be arrested."

"Oh, please hold."

Hmm, since I'm not registered, am I a student covered by the handbook and the Dean of Students? Didn't think of that, did you? Probably should have just called the Public Defender.

"Mr. Francisco," Dr. Sheldon's familiar voice came through the phone, "I was just talking to the registrar about you. Do you mind coming up to my office and let's see if we can get this straightened out?"

"Okay, should only take five to ten minutes and I'll be there."

"Great, I'll be expecting you."

Awe, he's a smooth one. Going to have to be careful. Wonder if he ever gets ruffled. That day in Wheat's room, he looked like he might lose it for a moment. So disappointed when Mike produced that note giving him permission to take that calculator home for the night. Wonder how this is going to go.

I arrived at Doctor Sheldon's outer room. "Hi. I'm Kim Francisco. I think I'm expected."

His secretary stopped typing, turning from her typewriter to look at me over her desk, "Yes. Hang your coat on the stand and I'll announce you.

Trying to be cool, hard to do taking off a heavy parka, I tried to casually add it to the other coats on the coat stand in the corner, which being over weighted with coats on one side, fell over. I caught it as it fell, ending up with both arms full of coats and the stand. I reset the stand and distributed the coats so they balanced each other and the coat tree stood proudly.

This never happens to James Bond when he tosses his hat on to Money Penny's hat stand.

With a suppressed laugh, the secretary said, "Go right in."

Hope I made her day. Smiling at the secretary, I stepped into the dreaded office of the Dean of Students.

"Have a seat," the tall well-built man behind the desk said with his deep smooth voice.

Here we go, stay calm; Harris isn't the problem, it's the registrar.

"Sounds like you forgot to register and owe a lot in late payments. I'm sure we can work out a payment schedule that will make everyone happy."

"No sir, I did not forget. As this receipt clearly shows, the registrar refused my payment and registration. The late registration fees are her problem, not mine."

Looking up from the copy of my registration's front page with the handwritten, signed receipt in the margin, he said, "I suppose the original is in a safe place because you don't trust us."

"I trust you, just thought multiple copies would be needed. The registrar already kept one. Although, she threw it away."

"I see. She said she couldn't register you because you had conflicting classes."

"Yes sir, I'm taking Vertebrate Biology and Scientific Sampling, and the lectures are at the same time. Luckily, the labs are at different times. Since they both are only offered in the spring and I wanted to graduate this year, I needed to take them both," I explained.

"But you can't do that."

"Pardon me, sir, but you seem to have forgotten that if you have the permission of both instructors and your advisor, you can take classes simultaneously. As these copies of the signed and dated permissions show, I had permission when I registered."

He looked at the permission slips and frowned, then regained his composure and asked, "Will you wait in the reception area while I make some calls?"

"Yes sir, I brought a book. Those copies are yours." I stepped out of the room. *Hope I'm not overdoing the sir, but Dad said it always helps. Wonder who he's calling. Getting ahold of everyone in the file could take a while. Always fun rereading the Lord of the Rings trilogy; this next chapter is the first with the Ents, my favorites.*

Dr. Shelden called his secretary to let me back in. I saved her the trouble and stepped to the door, retaking my seat in front of his desk.

"You really should have called me or Dr. Dean when this happened, so you share some of the responsibility. We will only charge you half of the late fee and call it even."

"Hmm." *She told me she was the final word and there was no appeal. I'm a know nothing student, well, not quite true, but she was the person in authority and should have known the rules so I don't think half the responsibility is mine.* "No, sir. I went to a lot of trouble to find out if I could and how to take both classes. I then jumped through all the university's hoops, which while designed for my protection do seem to assume I'm incapable of knowing my own abilities. As I assume you found out, I'm doing well in both classes. Unless of course the University's goal in collecting late fees is to raise funds, rather than simply encourage timely registration. I don't think processing my registration now is going to cost the university much. Certainly not even half of the ridiculous late fee the registrar is asking for. If that is your best offer, then I think I should talk to a public defender and write a letter to the Polar Star. and News Miner." *Rats, left an opening for more negotiation.*

Dr. Sheldon looked down at the copies from my file, looked up and smiled, "I told the registrar that you wouldn't pay late fees, but I promised I would try to collect something, so we didn't set a precedent."

"How's a buck sound?"

He shook his head as he pulled a file from the file drawer in his desk. "Let's forget late fees. This was an administrative error that needs to be corrected. We'll finish calculating your fees before I send you back to finish registration."

"Okay." *Can't believe it. You can fight city hall.*

"Can you hand me your original registration, please?"

"Here it is," I said, whipping it out of the file and handing it to him. He had to tug it a little before I let go. *Are copies enough? Is this a trick to get the original?*

He must have seen the thought in my eyes or in my slow release because he said, "This isn't a trick, we just need to adjust these changes on the charge sheet." He laid it down on his desk and started following down with his pen.

"Okay, resident tuition. Check."

"Late fees. None."

"Student Fee. Check."

"Dorm Fee?"

"Yes, need to charge me for a single" *Won't mention Marsha.*

"How did you get a key without registering?"

"Showed up at night, half frozen, after driving the highway with a broken windshield. They were expecting me since I registered last fall, so they gave me a key. Guess no one told the RA to throw me out." *Hope this doesn't get her in trouble.*

He wrote a Post It and continued, "Meal ticket." He opened the file he had gotten out earlier. *Oh no! Someone kept track of the times I snuck in.* "This will surprise you, but meal ticket is like a mortgage, you're not a business major and probably haven't had a mortgage yet. In any case, the first meal costs twenty-seven dollars and eighty-seven cents squared; the last meal is ten cents." He held up a table with dates and descending prices, then lay it back down, placing a small ruler under the day before. Then he began entering the numbers below into an adding machine. *Wow, he must do a lot of bookkeeping, he's fast. Could use him doing fish tickets!*

"There, the remaining meals comes to two-hundred and fifty-six dollars and forty cents." He crossed out the nine-hundred and fifty-six dollars that was preprinted on the sheet and wrote in the new lower figure.

I gulped. *Feeling guilty and dumb now. The meal ticket, the most expensive item on the registration fees page* (before late fees), *had completely slipped my mind. Guess I won't get to make up for meals snuck out to me and Marsha. Now I feel guilty about cheating the university. It's really cheating the damn people with the food service contract. Yeah, they don't deserve what they charge. I still feel bad.*

"There, look that over. If it seems fair to you, take it back to the registrar's office and settle up. You do still have your tuition?" Dr. Sheldon asked.

"Yes sir. This is fair. Sorry for all the trouble. Next time, I'll be sure to get it settled on registration day." I shook his outstretched hand and fled towards the door. *Almost said more than fair. Crap, I feel like a thief. Stop, get your coat. Marsha is even cleaning up my thoughts. Last year, I would have thought fuck. What a windfall! I'll have to timber the house at Woods Hole. Take Marsha out someplace really nice. Do I know any really nice places? The Octagon out on Goldstream. Never been there, couldn't afford it.*

Without noticing the trip, I found I had crossed the campus and was unzipping my coat as I entered the registrar's office reception area. As I stepped up to the service bar, the receptionist left. saying to no one and everyone: "I have a class. See you tomorrow."

Smiling at the receptionist's back and me, Carol rose from her desk and walked over to the reception bar. When close enough for me to hear, she whispered, "She's really on the war path after that last call. Everyone is finding something else to do somewhere else. She specifically said she didn't want to see you!" Returning to a normal tone of voice she asked, "How may I help you Kim?"

My face was on fire with embarrassment. *Wish I had Wheat's composure. He would bellow his presence loud enough to be her in the private office. You don't, so just get this settled.* "Hi, Carol. Sorry for all the trouble. Here's my fee schedule Harris approved." (To his face he was Dr. Sheldon, otherwise around campus he was Harris, and everyone knew who that was.)

She read down the page, her smile getting bigger. "How did you get off with no late fees? That's amazing. No wonder she's so mad. You better give me your check and get out of here before she finds a gun." Carol was really enjoying this.

Wonder what would have happened between us if I hadn't met Marsha. Probably nothing Kim, you didn't even think of her till you saw her again this year. I finished writing a check for the new amount and handed it to Carol. "Guess I get to graduate after all."

"I'm graduating this year too."

"Great, be at least one person I know. Seems like most of my friends graduated last spring. Sorry I've stirred up such a hornet's nest."

"Don't tell anyone, but I'm enjoying it. Well, see you at graduation if not before."

"Yeah, bye." I left and walked down the long hill to Lathrop Hall and my room. *Wow, nice to have money again. Already saved 10% when I was paid, so this is all for spending.*

CHAPTER FIFTEEN

❦

BACK TO EMMONAK

Life was good, thanks to the windfall, my job in Woods Hole, and Marsha's job with a local dentist. Geiger called and needed someone early to help put in the Flat Island Test Fishery site and set up the Emmonak office, so my future was assured for a few months. As the semester drew to an end, we found a basement apartment just a couple of blocks from the Sharp's, so Marsha would have a place to live while I was gone. We weren't looking forward to the separation but realized if Fish& Game became my career as planned, it wouldn't be the first nor last time.

Graduation was exciting. I was officially an adult, again. It's interesting the number of times that happens in our society: first communion, high school graduation, eligible for draft, becoming a voter, drinking age, then college graduation. We were discussing this at a graduation party: had we finally made it or did adulthood still have to wait for marriage, permanent job, and children? Many years later, Charlie Lean would end the discussion with a letter telling me he was finally an adult since he had a permanent job, mortgage, wife, and child. I always look forward to his Christmas letter.

The big disappointment at graduation was the commencement address. It was given by James Mitchener, an author I admired and dreamed of meeting one day. It was a boring twenty minutes of platitudes without a single original thought. His books lost their appeal for me afterwards. The most important thing was Marsha being there, glowing in her pride and happiness for me.

A day later, we were saying goodbye till August at the Fairbanks Airport as I left for Anchorage and Bethel. Mike Readon, Flat Island Crew Leader, and friend, picked me up at the Bethel Airport. We returned to the Bethel office compound overlooking the Kuskokwim River and filled the pickup with a load of gear. Back to the airport, and we dropped that load and went to Swanson's grocery store and bought a couple weeks' worth of groceries for Flat Island and Emmonak. Unlike the previous summer, the Bethel storage shed wasn't filled with year-old canned goods. Although I knew there were several cans of Spaghetti O's waiting in Bethel, it would be their third year.

Fritz was starting his first year as the Kuskokwim Area biologist since Mr. Yanagwa had transferred to a new position. This gave me hope that being a fish ticket editor in Emmonak would lead to better things. It and my graduation had already led to a promotion from Fisheries Tech III to Fisheries Biologist I, and a nice pay bump. I would later learn that a lawsuit by some FT's had won them overtime pay. The old slave labor form, "I'll work till the job is done" was history. FBI were still classified as professionals, not qualified for OT. It had become cheaper to hire FBIs than FTIIs. Luckily, I never measured my success in dollars, but happiness and satisfaction.

With the truck filled with groceries, we headed to the airport again, stopping at the F&G compound, and picking up the new Kuskokwim fish ticket editor so he could return the truck. We boarded the Emmonak-Mountain Village-St. Mary's mail flight, just us, the pilot, and lots of freight.

We disembarked in Emmo, happy to see the three-wheeler and wagon guy there to help us with our gear. The mail bag came out first and he grabbed it and headed across the bridge to the PO, a two-minute walk. We watched him as he handed off the mailbag and disappeared into the village.

"What the hell?" Mike said to me.

"Guess he has more important things to do today," I said as I took another box from the pilot and added it to our pile.

Mike turned to take the next box, but the pilot was down to the new 40 hp outboard. I joined Mike, catching the outboard as the pilot slid it out. As we set it on the ground, Mike stood, closing the freight door, and saying, "Have a good flight" to the pilot.

We watched the takeoff, then looked around. We were alone, standing next to a pile of freight a half mile from the warehouse F&G rented from AC.

Mike said, "We have lots of friends in town. As soon as they see us carrying this 40 horse, someone will come help. Let's go."

We put our packs with our personal gear on, then we grabbed a side of the handlebar across the front of the outboard. Side by side, the outboard between us, we staggered across the bridge following the road along the river, talking about nothing. "Time out, my arm's had it." I was using my left weak arm for our carry. We stopped, switching sides, and started out again.

"We should have seen someone by now," Mike said.

"Yeah, the place seems deserted. Must be a wedding or a funeral going on," I added.

"Hope it's a wedding. Wonder why no one has come to help us yet?" Mike asked the universe.

I said, "Hey we can get rich with a country western song."

"Huh."

No one's around when you're carrying a 40 horse.
They all hide in their house till the work is done.
They leave you alone, even our sweeties are gone—

I was interrupted by Mike. "You should be on the stage, and there's one leaving in a minute and thirty seconds if you don't stop!"

"Awe, you don't like country. Should I try rock?" I said in my best hurt voice.

"Fuck you."

"Please, somebody?"

"Sleeping with my back to the wall tonight. You've only been gone one day," Mike said.

"Break, let's switch." We switched sides, again, and our journey continued. The conversation ranged from profound to profane and we picked that outboard up I don't know how many times. Finally, we reached the AC store. We both got sodas and I picked up a Milky Way.

Mr. Moses gave Mike the key. I didn't see Irene behind the counter or stocking shelves; I almost asked Mr. Moses but didn't. *Hell, you have Marsha. No reason to bring up that bad memory of Tommy Jr.'s death. Just let it go.*

Outback at the outboard, we finished our sodas, and I finished my candy bar when we picked the outboard up for the last fifty yards. We unlocked the warehouse and found a fuel tank that still had gas in it. Picking it up, Mike shouted from the attic, "Hope it hasn't turned to varnish!"

"Have you ever actually seen that happen? I've only seen them collect water. George made sure we put stabilizer in them all so it should be alright. He wasn't always the greatest company, but he sure knew his stuff."

"Good. Wouldn't want to row that test fish boat to the airport. Had enough exercise for one day," Mike said as he came down the ladder after lowering the gas can. We left the haul rope hanging from the roof rafter since we would need it again later as we lowered gear out of the attic.

We went outside, opened the gas can, and poured out a small amount. It looked and smelled like gas, so we set it next to the new forty and headed to the boatyard west of the warehouse. There we located the test fish skiff, not looking as shiny and new as it had after Mike and Allo painted last summer before putting it up for storage.

We flipped it over with some effort since wooden boats are heavy. We set the small logs that had held it off the ground for air circulation in front of the bow, then prowled the boat for other potential logs not in use to convert into rollers for the skiff.

Laid out in front, we pushed the skiff's bow up on the first roller. Once we got it going, I pushed on the stern while Mike grabbed the rollers as they came out from underneath the skiff and moved them to the front to extend our line of rollers. Things went smoothly until we left the level boatyard and started down the bank to the river. As gravity took over, my job switched from pushing to guiding the boat to the next roller and braking the boat to keep it from overrunning the rollers before Mike got the next one in place.

As always, when entering the water, it was too deep for a roller and too shallow to float the bow. We had anticipated this, and were working in our hip boots when the bow stuck in the bottom. We each stepped to a side, lifted the bow, and pulled the boat forward. The forward half of the skiff afloat the wider stern was loosely grounded. We scrambled for the forty and carried it down, dropping it onto the transom.

While Mike tightened the outboards, mounting bolts onto the transom, I carried down the gas tank, hose, seat cushions, and oars. With the safety line fastened between boat and motor, Mike double checked that the drain plug was back in. Many a sailor has been embarrassed to discover during the first launch of the year the boat was sinking because the drain plug had been overlooked.

The new outboard took a little coaxing as they do; Mike had to pull the rope starter many times before it coughed to life. Once its lifegiving mixture of gas and oil was flowing, it ran smoothly. I pushed the skiff and Mike out onto the river. As I was climbing in over the bow, Mike goosed the engine, toppling me into the skiff. He laughed and I grumbled at this old joke.

Mike didn't believe in breaking the engine in; typically, not more than half throttle for the first hour then not more than three-quarters throttle for ten hours. He went all the way to full and headed upstream to the airport. We completed our long walk in about four minutes by boat and I climbed onto the steep bank at the end of the runway. We pulled the bow up on the bank, tossing out the anchor just in case the boat drifted off we could retrieve it.

It was early in the season. We were possibly the first people to climb the airport bank since the ice break-up, so the usual crude stairway wasn't started in the bank yet. Kicking with our toes, we put a start on a set of stairs into the mud bank as we climbed to the airport. Once at our pile of gear, "our friend" with the three-wheeler and trailer returned, watching to be sure we didn't take anything out of the pile not tagged for Fish& Game. After our first trip, Mike said, "Let's get smart about this, you stay on top and toss stuff down to me. Otherwise, one of us will slip and fall in the river."

"Good idea." I turned and climbed back up our "stairway".

This did go quicker, plus I had the fun of pretending a heavy box was light and getting to watch if I surprised Mike when he caught it. Nothing broke, and the air freight guy left on his three-wheeler. Mike and I spent the rest of the day bringing the test fish gear down out of the warehouse attic. We also turned over the big double wide cargo skiff. It had started out to be a test fish boat, but was too big for the job, so took on a new role as cargo skiff.

CHAPTER SIXTEEN

FLAT ISLAND

The Yukon had become so wide you couldn't see the far bank. Even the south bank we had been following had become a maze of sloughs and distributaries, every ice break up and flood leaving their own mark. Reardon was aiming the skiff towards the center of the largest channel, I assumed since no land was visible, and I was looking at the Bering Sea. I was watching the big freight skiff we were towing behind. It was an amazing spring day. The usual cloud cover was gone, nothing but blue sky. The sun was actually beginning to become oppressive. The previous summer there had only been one day like this and that was in July, not May.

Mike shouted over the engine, "There she is: Flat Island."

Looking over the bow, I could see a dark line on the river ahead of us. A look through the binoculars revealed a flat dark line with cylinders sticking up near the center. *Silos! You dummy, this isn't the Midwest. Those are the sand filled 55-gallon drums you'll be building the camp on. Remember your visit last summer?*

I checked our tow again. After filling the big skiff, we had waded out with the floors: 4' x 8' sheets of⅝' marine plywood nailed onto 2' x 4' stringers with 2' x 4' cross braces on 24' centers. Once piled on the cargo skiff, we lashed them down forward to aft and starboard to port. It made a heavy, awkward load, but we had evidently done a good job balancing it, since it was towing straight and true. It was a little exciting when we slowed for any reason since the momentum of the loaded skiff caused it to ride forward, threatening the tow skiff and its occupants, Mike, and I. This was when I earned my money by fending it off with the big oar we carried. The rest of the trip, I just had to watch to make sure we didn't lose the skiff or any of its contents, which had been easy on such a windless, warm day.

The mooring posts had survived break up, so we quickly secured the two skiffs. Then we stood up straight, stretching our backs, viewing Mike's home for the next seven weeks. The highest objects were the collection of sand-filled 55-gallon drums, otherwise there was virtually no relief; the island was scoured flat by the river. The grass and forbs growing in the sand made it just barely an island. It still regularly went underwater on high tides.

"Lots of driftwood this year, should be plenty for the fish camp and us. Let's get these drums moved into position," Mike said.

I grabbed two, eight-foot 2x8's from the skiff and the 24' level from the tool box. The ice had shifted the drums, so Mike was studying them to figure out which one would make the "golden" corner. That is, using it as a starting point required moving the minimum number of drums the smallest distance. Starting from the chosen corner, we began wrestling and rolling the drums into two 12' x 16' rectangles with the drums on four-foot centers. Using the 2' by 8', level and shovel we added and subtracted sand (really just glacial silt for you geologists and civil engineers) from underneath the drums until the surface was level.

Mike interrupted our conversation comparing fiancées to say, "Done, and I have to take my shirt off. First time we've had such a nice day we worked in t-shirts."

"Yeah, packing those floorboards up from the boat and putting them on these drums is going to be hot work," I said as I added my wool shirt to the growing pile of clothing. "You know, considering the vast difference in their backgrounds, it's surprising how similar our girls are. Strong argument for nature over nurture," I said, walking down to the boats.

Mike took a seat on the bow of the test fish skiff, and I sat on the bow of the cargo boat to put our hip boots on. Then we wadded out alongside the cargo boat and its load of floors. We began untying the lines holding the floorboards in place on the boat, tossing the end back and forth over the boat, endeavoring to hit the other guy on the head with the rope end. The fore and aft, port to starboard lashing undone, we each grabbed the end of the top floorboard, carrying it to shore and up to the foundations we had built with the drums. Dropping it into place we returned for the next and the next…. This all was done to a steady drone of friendly insults, profanities. and further discussion of our fiancées.

The similarities were amazing considering Nita was Yup'ik, raised in the village of Kotlik, located on the northern most distributary of the Yukon River's mouth. Marsha had been born in Minneapolis (don't forget) but raised in Des Moines. On the surface, the only thing they had in common was the Roman Catholic Church. Both were shy about noisy sex. Didn't understand the banter us guys used between friends. Both were beautiful, but seemingly unaware of it, that is unlike many (certainly not all) babes, they didn't expect special consideration based on their looks. "You know, Mike, probably a good thing they are like that. Otherwise, they probably wouldn't have looked twice at us."

"Speak for yourself, women can't resist me."

My laughter was all the response Mike needed or wanted. We reassembled the tent frames, screwing them firmly to the floors. Then we put up the first tent, which would house the kitchen, storage area, and work space if needed during bad weather.

We took a break for a soda and some peanut butter and jelly on pilot bread. "Became fond of this stuff last summer, but pilot bread is a little hard to find in Fairbanks. Finally found it at Sportsmen's Mall, in with the dehydrated food," I told Mike.

"Yeah, I could have told ya that. Hey, did you ever notice we only pass each other now and then on campus? We both have the same major. Why don't we have any classes together?"

"That is odd, now that you mention it. Plus, you seem to hang out with your upper dorm friends. Busy looking down on us lower dorm people," I added.

"Don't want to get contaminated by you jocks. But you're not a jock, are you?" Mike asked.

"Naw, just live with them. I've always been the last one chosen all my life. Although I'm on a couple of Lathrop's intramural teams because they need a semi-warm body to make the minimum number."

Mike laughed. "Let's get the canvas on. No wind today. Sunshine wishing, I packed shorts for the first time. We're going to set a new record for putting the camp up."

I finished the last swallow and joined Mike unfolding the canvas wall tent. The one on top we were unfolding was dingy grey with age and had several holes and other damage from age.

"We use this beater for the cook tent. Think Geiger is going to have spring for a new one. This one has about had it. I'll have to put a note on the inventory for him," Mike said.

"Yeah, I like my solid roof during the storms. Damn, but sometimes I think that sheet metal siding is going to come off in the wind."

"You should listen to one of these tents in the wind. It really howls. Last year, when that high tide and storm hit together, the whole island went way under water. The whole fish camp next door moved in with us. Gals took over the cook tent, kept everybody fed and the coffee hot, but we had to use a boat to go between tents," Mike said.

"What did you guys do?"

"Played poker. I lost my shirt."

Laughing, we spread the canvas onto the frame. Mike started tying the canvas down on the right side and I on the left. I lost the race to the center of the back wall. A welcome cool breeze hit our sweaty t-shirts as we headed for the year-old sleeping tent. "Hey, this is nice more comfortable than the sauna," I said.

"Yeah, but if we were in Emmo, we'd be down in the bathhouse in the sauna."

"We talked about that at one of the bull sessions in the dorm last year. What would an alien think if he saw the little dorm fridge in a warm room while it was forty below outside the window?"

"Glad I don't live down there. Your thoughts are too deep."

As we unfolded the second tent, the pleasant breeze turned into a chilling wind and we both paused to put our shirts back on. We repositioned the ladder and Mike climbed to the rear peak. I handed him the rear-top of the tent, but a gust of wind ripped it from our fingers. "Fucking, A."

"I'll get it."

"God bless it."

A gale force wind suddenly arose, wrapping me in the part of the tent, the rest of the tent wrapped around the ladder. My head was wrapped in canvas, I could hear Mike's muffled voice shouting, "Damn it, get the ladder!"

Where's the fucking ladder? I was trying to turn my back to the wind and pull the canvas down far enough to see, when I heard Mike shout, "Oh shit!" followed by the rattling crash of the ladder and every profanity Mike knew.

My hands finally found the top of a fold in the canvas pulling it down so I could see. The ladder was on the ground, the canvas was all wrapped around me and streaming out downwind as it tried to topple me over.

Mike was on the ground, sitting up and swearing. *Doesn't seem to be hurt.* I kind of swiveled on my downwind leg, which let the canvas unwrap me and stream off downwind. I dropped down on my knees, pinning the canvas to the ground. Still swearing, mostly at the wind but saving a little for me and the tent, Mike crawled over and pinned the nearest piece of canvas under his hands. Mike finally stopped swearing and went silent.

After a long pause, during which the only sound was the cold wind howling in my ears, I asked, "Are you okay?"

"No, I'm not fucking okay. I just fell off a ladder. Damn wind. How are we going to get this tent up?

Um, with great difficulty. Not the answer. "How about finding the upwind edge and let the wind put it over the frame?"

Mike paused thoughtfully. "You have half an idea. Let's see if we can get this tent to the upwind side."

We were thankful the Candid Camera crew wasn't there. It took forever to find the edges of the tent which the wind would get under and flap and wrap the canvas, defeating what progress we had made refolding it. With it streaming downwind, we finally got the right side onto the bottom, the door at the front, and the whole thing folded accordion-like in a pile streaming out downwind. I was sitting at the upwind end and Mike was sitting on it about two-thirds of its length downwind to keep it from flapping. Not sure how we caught our breath since we were busy using up all our swear words. I even think for the sake of variety I used my mother's gem, 'this discombobulated steam pipe!' Mom taught first grade and tried not to swear.

Mike said, "Let's pick it up."

"I think it would be best if you picked up the middle there first. I'll keep this end down so the wind can't get underneath."

"Okay." Mike slid one arm under and the other over the tentstreamer we had created. He sat up onto his knees and said, "Lift your end."

Getting a firm grip, I started for my knees, but once in motion I didn't want to waste the momentum and ended up squatting on my feet, prepared to throw myself on the canvas if the wind blew it away. Nothing happened, except the wind tugging hard on the canvas, so Mike stood up.

I rose to my feet, saying, "Let's go," and stepped upwind towards the front of the tent frame. The new location was actually in the "lee" of the previously erected cook tent, which helped a little, but the wind was so strong as it poured through the drums, around and over the tent, that we found ourselves in an area filled with williwaws that tugged and pulled the canvas in every direction.

Mike picked-up the 12' step-ladder, setting up the back of the tent frame even with the ridge pole. I got to take a break by lying down on the canvas pinning as much of it to the ground as I could. Then we each stood on an end of the canvas, digging down through the folds until we found the bottom corner front and back. We then leaned against the corner drums with our shoulders as we pinned the corners under the drums.

Returning to the corners on the top of the pile, we began unfolding the canvas up and over the frame; of course, immediately discovering the flaw in our plan. Mike was going to need some slack to get around the corner to the ladder. The canvas was brought to life by the williwaws, making it difficult to keep under control as we worked it around the corner. Mike started climbing the ladder, which allowed me to payout canvas unto the tent frame as I also worked my way forward. The wind was cooperating as planned and pinning the canvas against the drums and the side and roof of the frame.

As I reached the door, the next tricky part began. I had to climb up the steps to the top of the floor, then let Mike, the wind, and I guide the canvas over the top. We then would tie the downwind site down to the frame and return to the upwind corners, taking them out from under the drums. Then tie it to the floor, run around, and pull the far wall down and tie it to the floor. Simple, right?

No. As we started the canvas over the ridge pole, the wind whipping around the cook tent filled the canvas like it was a sail. I'm uncertain exactly in which order the following events happened, but the bulging tent-turned- sail knocked Mike and the ladder over, Mike lost his grip on the canvas, I lost my grip on the canvas (we never decided who lost their grip first, this is my version, so Mike did). The corners came out from under the drums. The canvas slammed into the side of the tent frame, bending it out of square as it then flew off into the sand and grass of Flat Island.

I didn't have to ask Mike if he had been hurt in the fall since people with broken bones couldn't join me running to catch the canvas. We tackled the rolling canvas, wadding into an odd-shaped package that defied any shape I had learned in geometry. Leaning against the wind, each of us carrying an end, we returned to the relative shelter on the lee side of the cook tent.

We sat down on the canvas wad and finished our obscene description of what had happened and of each other since clearly one of us was at fault for the failure of such a perfect plan. The blue sky had disappeared, and the darkening clouds promised rain.

We agreed to disagree on what happened and untangled and refolded the canvas. Then we sat on it spitballing ideas for putting it onto the frame in the gale. Mike's eyes suddenly lit up with inspiration. "Geiger's budget can damn well afford two new tents." He got up and marched determinedly to the tool box as I sprawled out onto the canvas. He returned with a hammer and bag of two headed 10 penny nails. (We used them on the frame, the top head made them easy to pull out. We reuse the hole in the frame.) Finding the front corner of the inside (facing the cook tent) tent wall, he nailed the corner to the floor. He then repeated nailing the tent to the frame and floor all the way to the back.

Using the ladder stairway and a chair I got from the boat, I went to work with a second hammer. Probably a half hour later, we had nailed the tent to the 2x4 frame and floor. It barely shuddered in the wind.

We unpacked the rest of the gear, dividing it between the two tents depending on its use. The gear was mostly packed into the wooden crates, the crates were recycled from the ones two five-gallon cans of white gas for the stove came in. Stacked on their sides, the boxes made instant shelves. We had a small, mismatched set of chairs, one OD green steel office chair, picked up at an army surplus sale or perhaps left over from the transition from Alaska's territorial days to statehood almost fifteen years ago. Less rugged but more comfortable and transportable were two folding deck chairs. A small steel table, probably surplus, went into the center of the kitchen tent. The three-burner white-gas stove went on one end with a set of box shelves against the rear of the tent that held the plates, mixing bowls, and canned goods. Just inside the left tent door was the Homelite chainsaw with bar-oil, 2-gallon gas can, and extra cans of oil to mix with the gas. The tool box, crosscut, and bow saw were in the right corner, the saws hanging from nails in the frame.

Next was the radio. This was the second year Flat Island had one of the new field radios, which were generally despised. Unlike the older, albeit more delicate tube radios, these new radios were more compact transistor jobs that couldn't be tuned into shortwave, AM, or other channels and bands. They came with a dial that allowed a choice between four channels. One the channel assigned to ADF&G, another for Alaska's Department of Transportation, and another for the Alaska Department of Public Safety. I don't recall the fourth being assigned, I think it was just a space for another channel if it were ever needed. As a result of these new radios, you had to bring your own AM transistor radio for entertainment. Being creative, the field camps did go on the air after radio schedule to gab with one another on the ADF&G channel.

Mike and I set up the ladder behind the tent again, with me holding it firmly on the ground so it couldn't blow over. Mike climbed to the top and screwed the whip antenna base into the end of the ridge pole. The wind made the antenna live up to its name, but Mike made it up and down without incident. We pushed the antennae's cable under the bottom of the canvas and into the tent. Back inside we finished connecting the radio to the antenna and battery. Surprisingly, we caught the very end of the A-Y-K radio schedule.

"KE 6628 Bethel this is KE6628 Flat Island. Testing, can you hear us? Over," Mike said.

Mike Jonrowe's (just Jonrowe after this to many Mikes in this story) voice came back, "KE6628 Flat Island, this is Bethel, read you five by five. Weren't expecting you until tomorrow. Bethel. Over."

Grinning, Mike replied, "You think we were just laying around doing nothing? Flat Island. Over."

"Just didn't expect you to be ready so soon. Will you have a test fish report in the morning? Bethel. Over."

Mike held the mic to his chest, unnecessary since he hadn't keyed it on, swearing about the unappreciative supervisors who expected miracles. Then keying the mic, he answered, "No! We'll try to get the nets in tomorrow morning. If we have time. KE6628 Flat Island. Out."

"Sorry, Flat Island, Geiger just wanted to know. KE6628 Bethel. Out."

We chatted while I fixed supper and Mike whittled on a block of wood that with a little imagination you could begin to see the shape of a ladle, or in this case, an *ipuun* (Sounded like nippon, when Mike said it.). He explained it was a traditional Yup'ik gift between fiancées.

Later, after the storm had blown itself out, I woke up to the sound of belugas blowing out in the channel. A relaxing sound that Mike always said was one of the benefits of Flat Island.

CHAPTER SEVENTEEN

FIRST KING

The alarm clock sitting on the stack of boxes Mike had converted into a nightstand at the head of his bed began ringing at seven-thirty.

I poked my head out of my sleeping bag and tried to turn it off with a dirty look and even dirtier thought. Just as I was going to climb out to kill this evil thing, a hand appeared from the top of Mike's sleeping bag, reminiscent of Thing on the Munster's. Just enough arm followed to reach the alarm clock and turn off its defending din. On its way back into the sleeping bag, the hand turned on the radio to warm it up.

I sunk back into my sleeping bag. Before I could fall asleep, the radio called "KE6628 Eek Island, KE6628 Eek Island this is KE6628 Bethel." Eek answered. Bethel repeated its call to Eek. Eek answered. Bethel repeated its call to Eek. Eek answered. Bethel signed off with Eek. "Calling KE6628 Flat Island," the hand once again appeared out of the sleeping bag, unhooked the microphone, and pulled it back into the sleeping bag. The sleeping bag began mumbling. Jonrowe's cheery voice came back, "KE6628 Flat Island you sound under the weather."

No, he's under the sleeping bag.

Mumble, mumble.

"You can hear Eek?"

Mumble, mumble.

"Good, Geiger will be happy to hear the nets are out. Can you check with Eek to see if they need anything?"

Mumble mumble. Mumble mumble.

"Eek back, just a radio that works!"

He sounds unhappy.

Mumble.

"Eek out with Flat Island."

Mumble mumble.

"Bethel back to Flat Island, anything else?"

Mumble mumble.

"Bethel out and standing by."

The hand and mic appeared. After hanging up the mic, the hand turned off the radio. Soon snores began coming from the sleeping bag.

I tried to go back to sleep but couldn't. My mind was active with story ideas, remembering Marsha and coffee. I quietly slipped out of my underwear and slipped into a fresh pair of shorts and t-shirt. It took more shorts than many of my coworkers, but I always tried to have enough underwear for every day. I had learned in Boy Scouts that clean underwear was almost as good as a shower. I hadn't lasted long in the contest to see who could wear their shorts the longest at Camp Mitigawa. Heard of a guy in the National Guard that wore the same pair for the entire 21 days of their training deployment.

I put the clothes on from yesterday, grabbed my notebook and the novel I was reading, moving quietly to the cook tent. I put together a pot of coffee, fired up the Coleman stove, and put the coffee on to percolate. I settled into a lawn chair and jotted down some notes. The first spurts of coffee came up into the glass viewer on top of the coffee pot. I turned the heat down and started reading. When the coffee reached a rich dark brown, I poured a mug full and put the coffee back on low heat. I settled in with my book. When I finished the first pot, I considered waking Mike, but quickly reconsidered it. He was the crew leader and had made it clear he liked to sleep in the morning.

"Is the coffee ready? How about bacon and eggs?" Mike interrupted my reading and first cup out of the second pot.

"Already had one pot, but this one's ready," I said, standing and extending the pot. Mike stuck his mug out, which I filled. "I'm ready to eat. How do you like your eggs?"

"Scrambled."

We traded stories of other field camp breakfasts as I opened a can of Danish Bacon it was packed with lard and salt. I covered the cast iron frying pans bottom with strips of thick bacon. As the bacon shrunk, making room, I added more until we each had six. Piling them to one side of the pan, I started cracking eggs into a small plastic bowl. "How many?"

"Ugh, three."

I mixed three eggs with a little condensed canned milk, which I then poured into the hot grease. "You like em wet or dry?"

"Wow, what service. Need to get you transferred down here. Wet."

Stirring the eggs, I answered, "Might be a nice change from fish tickets. Don't think Mike would like two beginners in Emmo again. Your eggs are ready." I slipped the spatula under the scrambled eggs in the center of the pan. Mike stuck out his pate, I put the eggs and six pieces of bacon on it.

Mike said, "I think it would do him good to spend more time there with the fishermen."

"They don't call him 'ears of stone' for nothing." I cracked three eggs into the hot grease. I like mine over easy. I had solved the turning them over problem the previous summer, the bacon left so much grease in the pan it was easy to use a spoon to pour hot grease over the yolk until you had a perfect over easy egg. Like Mike, I added some pilot bread to the breakfast. Mike liked strawberry preserves on his, I used honey.

After breakfast, I helped Mike with dishes. It was his turn since I cooked, but I wanted to be out on the water. Since the net and anchors were in the cargo skiff, we towed it out to test net site one and dropped the anchors with the orange sea-lion buoys. They were labeled ADF&G on one side and had Clarence's boat number on the other. During the open fishing periods, we pulled our nets, which were old fashioned tarred cotton, and Clarence put in his commercial nets, made from multifilament, which all commercial fishers used. One of their complaints about our test fishing was that we did it with old fashioned, tarred cotton nets. Multifilament was stronger, didn't rot, and caught more fish. It was difficult for commercial fishers of any culture to understand why we would use less effective gear. Our explanation that we wanted the catches to be comparable from year to year just didn't make sense. My recollection is that this was the last year the department used cotton twine nets since it wasn't manufactured any longer and worn-out nets couldn't be replaced.

Mike and I were stretching out the king (8-inch stretch net) net between the two anchors and buoys at site one. As Mike backed up the boat, I was paying out the nets float line on one side, and the lead line on the other. It's important that the float line and its corresponding lead line go out together to keep the net even and prevent twists. Mike, of course, was backing up as fast as possible to see if I could keep up.

"Look!" I shouted over the motor.

Mike slowed and his head turned to look out over the bow. About halfway between us and the buoy, the cork line was dancing.

"Oh boy. Fresh king for supper."

"This early it might be a late sheefish or maybe a burbot."

"No way, in king gear it would be a world record sheefish, and if it's a burbot, God help us."

We continued setting the net at a slower pace since we were both watching the bobbing cork line. I tied off the net, Mike dropped me in my seat, as he hit the gas. Just before reaching the bobbing corks, he slammed the motor in reverse and brought us to a halt alongside the moving floats. I reached down and began pulling up the net, feeling the strength of the salmon fighting the twine. I pulled a beautiful silver fish into the boat.

Grabbing it with one hand, I stretched to the struggling salmon and the piece of net holding it over the gunnel. Grasping the fish's head, I squeezed the gill rakers of the struggling fish closed. A simultaneous tug forward cleared the twine from the gills. I then pushed the head back through the net, freeing the fish. I dropped the fish into the middle of the boat and let the float line go over the side and back into the water. Mike handed me a well- worn club, about a foot long and I gave the struggling king a sharp rap on the head. All movement stopped as it became perfectly rigid, all the colors and marking becoming enhanced and perfect for a fleeting instant, then everything went dull with death.

I had noticed this phenomenon in every species of fish collected at the moment of death; they seem to be blessed with perfection.

Picking the salmon up by the neck and supporting its weight in my other hand, I held it up for Mike. "This is the size king that looks the best. About twenty pounds, sleek and streamlined, thick enough to show how powerful the muscles could be. Those really big ones seem to just get thicker with size, look weak and potbellied. Don't you think?" I asked.

"The big ones make really nice strips. Don't have the smokehouse done yet, so this one will be steaks for supper."

Mike was the practical subsistence fishermen, just thinking about how to turn the salmon into food. Mike, in anticipation of his first winter supporting a wife, was planning to work with Clarence at the fish camp next door to the test fish site and put up salmon strips for the winter. When a tender was available, the test fish were normally sold and the money deposited in the state's treasury. But until the first commercial fishing period, Flat Island would have nowhere nearby to sell the fish. In the past, they had been given to the subsistence fishing camp once Clarence's extended family arrived. This year Mike had asked—at least he said he had—sometimes forgiveness is easier than permission, so I wasn't certain, frankly didn't care. I much preferred the fish being used to being deep sixed. In tagging studies, where crews were paid to closely attend a single net, the fish were removed, tagged, and released quickly enough that there was extraordinarily little mortality. In the case of a set net test fishery, where a small crew had to check multiple nets after every incoming tide, very few fish were alive or healthy enough to be released. The crew usually got a little rummy since the tide precedes and recedes in its occurrence every day. The crew isn't working a shift so their bodies can adjust, a constantly changing schedule that comes from a tide book leaves your body confused.

We set the second, large mesh (king net) and a third, smaller mesh (6-inch mesh net) that would catch other species, chum primarily; occasionally a red salmon. No red salmon spawning streams had been found in the Yukon, so they were probably strays that wandered by on their way somewhere else. During the even numbered years, there were

"Yukon Flapjacks," pink salmon that spawned in some of the streams near the mouth of the river. Because of the mesh size used to target the larger chum and king salmon, they were almost always large male pinks that had already begun coloring up for the spawning streams. Male pink salmons' entire body changes for spawning with the jaws extending into toothed claws, the back arching up to expand the fish's profile. The expanded profile results in a loss of the normal fusiform (torpedo like) body to a flattened body, thus the nickname flapjack.

Back at camp, we gutted and headed the salmon; our neighbors, the terns, put on quite the display of acrobatic flight as we tossed the guts and head out into the water. Mike cut the salmon into steaks about an inch and a half thick. He came over to the campfire we had built up before we left and was now a bed of hot coals. While he staked the salmon, I nestled the heavy cast iron skillet into the coals. "Do you want butter, corn oil, or bacon grease?

"Neither," said Mike, "watch this," and he dropped a steak into the center of the pan where it began to sizzle. "These first kings must be going all the way to British Columbia to spawn. They're so fat they cook in their own oil."

After a few minutes, Mike flipped the nicely seared steak. "Give me your plate," he said after a few more minutes.

"You cooked. Don't you want to eat first?"

"Go ahead, I'll do my own."

The steak was perfect, seared on both sides, almost cooked all the way through but just a little pink in the middle. It was the best salmon I had ever had. Not sure if it was the location, freshness of the fish, or the quality of the fish, but I gobbled up the whole thing. Mike was eating his so I threw another on and cooked it for myself. Barely finished it, my eyes being bigger than my stomach.

Mike was napping and I was reading when a floatplane buzzed us. "Hey Mike Geiger and your new crewman are here," I shouted unnecessarily since the plane had woken Mike up. Kicking off my sneakers, I slipped into my hip-boots and walked down to the muddy shore of the island. The pilot coasted in just upwind of the big utility skiff. Once the meat grinder stopped spinning, I stepped out into the water and grabbed the upwind float and its bowline, guiding the plane into a gentle landing alongside the skiff.

Mike had made it from the tent to the skiff by this time so he held the door as Geiger unfolded his tall body out onto the float and stepped into the skiff. The biggest black briefcase that I'd ever seen that went everywhere with Geiger was handed out. Geiger took it and walked up onto shore using the skiff as a dock. A big duffle bag came next, followed by Eric Hoberg, a friend from college, who I greeted with "Hi, Eric!", which seemed to surprise him.

At the same time, Geiger asked the pilot if he wanted a short break on shore. "Nope," was the reply. Mike and Eric were introduced. Geiger handed two big yellow envelopes with mail and paperwork for Flat Island and Emmo. He came over to shore next to where I was standing in the water steading the plane. "Kim, everything going okay?"

"Yeah, this is paradise. Can I switch with Eric?"

"No, you get back to Emmo. Your new partner will be here in a couple days. Had to go to a wedding for something."

"Okay, I'll bring the utility skiff back after you leave."

"Good. Don't sink it."

"I'll try not to." *His sense of humor is so dry, not sure if he's teasing about my near drowning when the old office skiff fell apart in the middle of the Yukon or if he seriously is warning me not to lose anymore state property. I'll take it as a joke.*

Mike had climbed back into the skiff and plane. "I'll turn you around," He said to the pilot through his open window.

"Thanks."

I pushed the plane back as I turned it away from the skiff. Mike was grabbing the float struts and helping me turn the plane, which of course brought the tail cone right over his head. But it wasn't Mike's first round-up, so he ducked under grabbing the float struts on the other side like I had and we finished the turn. The pilot started the plane, Mike and I let go quickly, turning our backs to the prop as the pilot hit the power, sending a spray of water into our backs and Eric's face as he stood watching. *First lesson, don't watch a floatplane take off from the behind. Life like standing behind a manure spreader. Eric's probably never seen a manure spreader either.*

We walked up to the tent. I was already packed so Eric unrolled his sleeping bag on the second cot.

Mike said, "You never do anything without a cup of coffee first, do you Kim." He filled three mugs and broke out the pilot bread and toppings.

I sat on the log we used to split kindling on, Mike took the yard chair, and Eric sat on the big log that was drying before we made it into firewood. Eric passed on the pilot bread and coffee. Mike sent him into the sleeping tent to check the tide book, which you had to correct for your location. Mike filled him in on how it was done and he came up with high tide. Mike said, "Great, almost time to check nets."

"Sounds like work. I'll leave for Emmo," I inserted into the discussion.

"Eric, why don't you start the outboard so it can warm up? Kim and I will finish our coffee."

Eric excitedly headed for the skiff, eager for the new experience. We watched as he figured out how to lower the motor into the water. Then he pulled out the choke like Mike had mentioned and started pulling on the starter rope. Mike and I sat chucking, watching Eric's display of strength and stamina. "I hope he doesn't break the rewind," I said.

"Nah, it's new, he's just breaking it in good. Will have to teach him not to yank it all the way to the end like that."

"Hey, I finished my coffee. I'll go down and show him what's wrong. Dollars to doughnuts he didn't plug in the gas hose," I offered.

"Won't take that bet. Let him figure it out. You know out here a doughnut is a lot more than a dollar."

"Good point." I was pouring Eric's untouched coffee back in the pot and pouring myself a new mug. "How long are you going to let him keep trying?"

"I don't know, looks like he's getting tired."

Eric was taking a break from his labors but then switched arms, his right being tired, and continued abusing the starter and rewind with his left. When his left was finally tired, he got out of the boat and marched back to where we sat. "I thought you said that motor was brand new. It's no damn good. We'll have to send it back."

Mike was staring into his coffee mug, then like he saw it in the dregs, he asked, "Eric, did you plug in the gas hose and give the bulb a couple of squeezes?" (From the A-Y-K field manual written by Rae Baxter and filled with all kinds of practical advice. Summer temps were all given a copy to read.)

"Fuck, I forgot." Eric turned and returned to the boat and motor.

Mike was still staring into his mug smiling slyly, then as Eric reached the boat looked up at me, laughing. "These city kids who come out here thinking it's going to be a Disney movie. Guess that's why Rae wrote the manual."

"Yeah, wait till I have to teach mine how to edit fish tickets."

"How the hell do you stand doing that all summer?" Mike asked.

"Oh it's a lot of paperwork, but there is something satisfying about the horizontal row and vertical row agreeing."

Eric started the engine on the second try.

"Eric, remember fuel, spark, air, and they'll start almost every time," I quoted my father.

Eric said, "Huh."

Mike said, "I'll explain." He backed the skiff out and we parted, waving.

I loaded my gear into the utility skiff, hooked up the gas hose, and headed upriver to Emmonak. It was a beautiful, bluebird day. With only a gentle breeze, I enjoyed my long trip up river.

CHAPTER EIGHTEEN

MIKE CUBED

I spent a couple of days on my own in Emmonak. I set up Big Gray, the wonderful old tube radio with multiple bands to provide extra entertainment communication and checked in on the 4:30 radio schedule after Flat Island. The next couple of days, I set up the office so I could start selling licenses. Took the 25 hp off the utility skiff and put it on the office skiff. Handed out processor packets and renewed old acquaintances and made some new friends.

It was the routine morning radio schedule until Mike Jonrowe put Mike Geiger on, who told me he was flying out with another Mike, whose last name escapes me, to work in the office.

Geez, guess your name has to be Mike to get hired. We don't call Geiger Mike since he's the area biologist. Jonrowe is just a voice on the radio we call Bethel. Confusion will be here in the office. Guess they'll all have to go by last names to avoid confusion.

Geiger dropped the new Mike off; he and the pilot had coffee while he gave the completed processor packets. I gave him a cursory look. "They look good, but where's AC's?"

"The fisheries manager is coming in on the ship any day now, and he has to do the packet."

"Okay, good job getting the dot sheet ready. Sold any licenses yet?"

"Surprisingly, no. Everyone is going to wait till you announce the first opening. Maybe we should announce, then cancel, that would get 'em buying," I said.

"Yeah, and get you hung and the office burned to the ground," Geiger said with just a hint of a smile.

Wow, he's loosening up. Guess Readon was right, it just takes a while for him to get to know you.

Alarmed, Mike asked, "They wouldn't really riot and lynch us."

Geiger didn't say anything. I jumped in. "Nah, these are great people. Protection is always amazed at how clean our openings are. They hardly ever have to write a ticket. We did have a little excitement last Fourth of July. A nice young man got drunk and angry with AC. Took an axe to their helicopter. Poor kid missed a turn fleeing with his boat and was killed in the crash." I gave a brief account.

"How's fishing?" Mike asked.

"With a net, good. Complete waste of time with a rod," Geiger said.

"You mean there's no place to catch a fish?" Mike asked.

"After the fishing periods, when the processors start grinding the heads, it leaves a chum line in the river. The little old ladies catch some whitefish and suckers with hand lines. I suppose you could use a rod and reel. I never tried, didn't want to disturb the ladies."

Geiger brought us back on task. "Kim, this package of fish tickets is for the Bering Trader." He motioned to the cube of fish tickets shrinkwrapped laying on the table. He was refilling his briefcase. "Do you need anything else?"

"Nope, it's all on the shopping list I gave you."

Mike started unpacking in the bunk room; the pilot, Geiger, and I went down to the plane. I steadied the plane, turning my back to it when the pilot shouted "Clear" and started the engine. As I stepped ashore, the new office manager for AC met me asking, "When's the opening?"

"Not for a while, king run just starting."

"Good, the supply ship is at the mouth of the river waiting for the pilot. Supposed to be there today. We're not ready yet."

"You're safe. How are you fixed for fish tickets?"

"We have plenty."

We were walking back to the front of our office and the back of his. Seeing the rain barrel on the back of AC's office reminded me to ask,

"Last summer you guys let us use water from your rain barrel. Can we use it again this year?"

"I'll have to wait for the fisheries manager."

"Okay, talk to you later." I turned to the office and met Mike.

Mike was already at the bottom of the ramp leading into the office. "What was that about water?"

"Did you try ours yet?"

"No."

"You'll notice a strong chlorine smell and taste. I decanted the glacial silt out, then treated river water with Clorox to make it potable. The snowmelt and rainwater from their barrel tastes much better," I explained.

Making an unpleasant face he said, "Yuck. Hey, do you need me, or can I scout around the village?"

I looked at my watch. "The mail plane should have been here. Stop at the PO, it's next to the runway and check for any general delivery mail for the office or me. Otherwise, have fun. Nothing else to do today."

"Sounds like an easy job," Mike said.

"Don't worry. Once fishing starts, you'll pay it back in uncompensated overtime."

Mike started unpacking in the bunk room; the pilot, Geiger, and I went down to the plane. I steadied the plane, turning my back to it when the pilot shouted "Clear" and started the engine. As I stepped ashore, the new office manager for AC met me asking, "When's the opening?"

"Not for a while, king run just starting."

"Good, the supply ship is at the mouth of the river waiting for the pilot. Supposed to be there today. We're not ready yet."

"You're safe. How are you fixed for fish tickets?"

"We have plenty."

We were walking back to the front of our office and the back of his. Seeing the rain barrel on the back of AC's office reminded me to ask, "Last summer you guys let us use water from your rain barrel. Can we use it again this year?"

"I'll have to wait for the fisheries manager."

"Okay, talk to you later." I turned to the office and met Mike.

Mike was already at the bottom of the ramp leading into the office. "What was that about water?"

"Did you try ours yet?"

"No."

"You'll notice a strong chlorine smell and taste. I decanted the glacial silt out, then treated river water with Clorox to make it potable. The snowmelt and rainwater from their barrel tastes much better," I explained.

Making an unpleasant face he said, "Yuck. Hey, do you need me, or can I scout around the village?"

I looked at my watch. "The mail plane should have been here. Stop at the PO, it's next to the runway and check for any general delivery mail for the office or me. Otherwise, have fun. Nothing else to do today."

"Sounds like an easy job," Mike said.

"Don't worry. Once fishing starts, you'll pay it back in uncompensated overtime."

Mike started unpacking in the bunk room; the pilot, Geiger, and I went down to the plane. I steadied the plane, turning my back to it when the pilot shouted "Clear" and started the engine. As I stepped ashore, the new office manager for AC met me asking, "When's the opening?"

"Not for a while, king run just starting."

"Good, the supply ship is at the mouth of the river waiting for the pilot. Supposed to be there today. We're not ready yet."

"You're safe. How are you fixed for fish tickets?"

"We have plenty."

We were walking back to the front of our office and the back of his. Seeing the rain barrel on the back of AC's office reminded me to ask, "Last summer you guys let us use water from your rain barrel. Can we use it again this year?"

"I'll have to wait for the fisheries manager."

"Okay, talk to you later." I turned to the office and met Mike.

Mike was already at the bottom of the ramp leading into the office. "What was that about water?"

"Did you try ours yet?"

"No."

"You'll notice a strong chlorine smell and taste. I decanted the glacial silt out, then treated river water with Clorox to make it potable. The snowmelt and rainwater from their barrel tastes much better," I explained.

Making an unpleasant face he said, "Yuck. Hey, do you need me, or can I scout around the village?"

I looked at my watch. "The mail plane should have been here. Stop at the PO, it's next to the runway and check for any general delivery mail for the office or me. Otherwise, have fun. Nothing else to do today."

"Sounds like an easy job," Mike said.

"Don't worry. Once fishing starts, you'll pay it back in uncompensated overtime."

Mike started unpacking in the bunk room; the pilot, Geiger, and I went down to the plane. I steadied the plane, turning my back to it when the pilot shouted "Clear" and started the engine. As I stepped ashore, the new office manager for AC met me asking, "When's the opening?"

"Not for a while, king run just starting."

"Good, the supply ship is at the mouth of the river waiting for the pilot. Supposed to be there today. We're not ready yet."

"You're safe. How are you fixed for fish tickets?"

"We have plenty."

We were walking back to the front of our office and the back of his. Seeing the rain barrel on the back of AC's office reminded me to ask, "Last summer you guys let us use water from your rain barrel. Can we use it again this year?"

"I'll have to wait for the fisheries manager."

"Okay, talk to you later." I turned to the office and met Mike.

Mike was already at the bottom of the ramp leading into the office. "What was that about water?"

"Did you try ours yet?"

"No."

"You'll notice a strong chlorine smell and taste. I decanted the glacial silt out, then treated river water with Clorox to make it potable. The snowmelt and rainwater from their barrel tastes much better," I explained.

Making an unpleasant face he said, "Yuck. Hey, do you need me, or can I scout around the village?"

I looked at my watch. "The mail plane should have been here. Stop at the PO, it's next to the runway and check for any general delivery mail for the office or me. Otherwise, have fun. Nothing else to do today."

"Sounds like an easy job," Mike said.

"Don't worry. Once fishing starts, you'll pay it back in uncompensated overtime."

CHAPTER NINETEEN

❦

REMOTE MEDICINE

I was having a cup of coffee and listening to the radio schedule begin. "KE6628 Eek, KE6628 Eek, KE6628 Bethel…"

I will never forget those call signs. Sick of them already, and summer has barely started.

The two new single sideband radios in Bethel and Eek that were supposed to solve the communication problems still weren't working very well. I could hear both broadcasting 5x5, but they could barely hear each other. Eek broadcasted the test fishing results. Bethel would ask for them to repeat. Eek would come back, "Did you copy?"

Bethel would come back, "Did not copy, repeat". This sort of exchange seemed to go on and on. I got a fresh cup of coffee. The test fishing results finally were transmitted. *That's over. Now for Flat Island. Shit, Eek's trying to send a shopping list.* I leaned back. *Wonder if I should break in and offer to relay. Nah, the problem is Bethel, they have trouble hearing us.* Eek struggled through spelling out a shopping list a letter at a time. Sometimes Bethel got the letter, sometimes they asked for it to repeat. Sometimes Bethel was able to guess what was being spelled, sometimes not till the last letter.

"Bethel back, anything else."

"Yes, send penicillin." Almost a whisper, didn't speak as loudly as normal.

"Bethel back, didn't copy."

In a normal, broadcast volume, "We need penicillin." "Bethel back, you need what?"

Is Jonrowe just being mean, making him repeat, or did they really not hear?

"PENICILLIN! I NEED PENICILLIN!" Eek shouted into the mic.

"Bethel back, do you need pencils?"

Laughing as I tried to sip coffee, I sprayed the table with coffee.

Mike's laughter came from the bunk room.

Suddenly, the response broke through whatever atmospheric condition was blocking the transmission, "CLAP! I HAVE CLAP! SEND PENICILLIN!"

An amused voice replied from Bethel, "Roger, received you 5x5 that time." Anything else?"

"EEK OUT!"

"KE6628 Flat Island, this is KE6628 Bethel."

There was a long pause, Bethel tried again.

Reardon, still laughing, managed to choke out "Bethel...this is...Flat Island."

"Flat Island go ahead."

"Can't top Eek."

"Bethel to Flat Island, we need your test fish numbers."

There was another long pause as Readon regained his composure, then transmitted the test fish results. I dutifully copied them into the field manual.

CHAPTER TWENTY

PUBLIC ART

I had written up a little public service announcement while Mike was out exploring Emmo. That evening at six., I began the Commercial Fisheries radio show. I got on the CB channel 9, the call channel, and announced, "Switch to Channel 22 for Emmonak Fish report." I then repeated the announcement on the VHF radio. Then, with a mic in each hand, I read the short script. "The commercial fisheries office is now open in Emmonak. Commercial fishing will begin soon. Beat the rush and drop by to buy your license. We will be standing by on CB and VHF most of the day. Official announcements will be made at either eight-thirty in the morning or six o'clock in the evening daily. Fish and Game out and standing by."

"Fish game, when does fishing start?"

I answered, "This is Fish and Game in Emmonak. Right now, subsistence fishing only is open all the time. Subsistence nets will have to be out of the water twelve hours before the commercial fishing periods.

Right now, no commercial fishing periods have been announced. Fish and Game Emmonak standing by."

No one came back. I hung up the mics and listened to the radios for any further questions for us. I also turned KNOM up for some music and began reading my book. The chatter on the radios was in Yup'ik, so except for the occasional "fish game", Mike and I didn't understand the discussion.

"This is boring. Mind if I poke around in the attic?" Mike asked.

"You're welcome to it. But don't mix things up, mostly just subsistence survey gear up there now, but Readon always puts things away a certain way and gets pissed if it gets rearranged."

"Nothing else up there?"

"Yeah, a few odds and ends we don't use or that AC left up there. If you see something you think we can use, bring it down," I replied.

Mike went up the ladder and I settled into my book. The discussion on the radios was over. I heard some racket from the attic, sounded like Mike was moving some things over to the hatchway. There were some clinks and clangs, then Mike said, "Kim, come over to the ladder and take this stuff."

I marked my place in the book and went to the bottom of the ladder, looking up. A big, too big for any of the outboards, three bladed brass prop came down on a rope. On top of the brass prop was a slightly smaller four bladed steel prop. This continued as Mike had strung the collection of mismatched old props that had been used on AC's large tender boats. I had always admired the big brass one, it seemed so pretty, but I never thought of a use for it. I guided the rope full of props onto the floor. Mike followed them down on the ladder when I guided the last prop into a circle with the bib brass one in the center.

Mike stopped and looked at the circle. "Not bad, hope you don't mind but I think I can do better."

"Err, what are you going to do? These are AC's, can't imagine they would want them again, but I suppose one or two might still work if they chewed up the wheel on one of the tenders."

"Don't worry. I'm going to hang them on spikes in the wall. If they need one, they can just take it down."

"Okay. Do you want any help?"

"Not right now. I have to think about the design."

I returned to the radios and my book. Mike stood studying the blank wall between the topo map college and the ladder to the attic.

No one had called for us on the radio for over half an hour. I announced that we were switching to CB channel 9 and VHF channel 11, the two hailing frequencies for those channels.

Mike was drawing lines on a piece of paper. Then, holding the paper in one hand, he transferred the design to the wall but in an expanded size. Then with a hammer and spikes, he began adding the props. When he was finished he asked, "How's it look?"

I stood up and moved opposite of it. "Looks like a bass clef from my saxophone playing days, but since the big brass prop at the bottom isn't right, I guess it looks more like some critter on the bottom blowing a stream of bubbles."

"You're not into art, man. Doesn't need to look like anything, just needs to look cool."

"You're right there. I expect pictures and sculpture to look like something. It is pleasing to the eye, but I still think it looks like a clam blowing bubbles."

CHAPTER TWENTY-ONE

THE MUCUS CONSPIRACY

It was Mike's turn to fix supper. We had finished the fresh meat and veggies that had come on the plane with Mike. He was looking through the canned goods and boxed foods stored in the kitchen pantry shelves. I was writing a letter to Marsha when Mike said, "What the hell is the Mucus Conspiracy?"

I finished the paragraph I was writing and leaned back laughing. "Wow, those must be left over from last year. The Kuskokwim and Yukon staff thought they could stretch the budget by making a big joint food order that would arrive on the first barge into Bethel. One of Baxter's seasonal's got stuck with picking it all up at the waterfront and transferring it to the food warehouse in the Bethel compound. It was several pickup loads. As happens when you're doing something repetitive like stacking groceries, his mind began to wander. Being a conspiracy nut, he noticed that most of the canned and dehydrated foods were starchy or slimy or both.

According to Readon, but I think it was second hand, the cases of SpaghettiOs finally broke him, and he came to the realization that the food choices were designed to create mucus. Since mucus is found in the soft areas of the body, clearly mucus softens people, both mentally and physically. Which is the reason the diets provided in institutions are rich in starch and other mucus producing food. The conspirators are trying to make us more compliant through our diet. He made an effort to save us by spending his free time labeling the dangerous foods."

Supper excluded the labeled foods that night.

The next morning, Mike set to work writing on the wall in the space between the sculpture and the map of the Delta. I was impressed with his calligraphy, which is hard with just a magic marker and an unlined wall. Titled, "THE MUCUS CONSPIRACY", it was an interesting very short story on how "they" were planning on taking over the world by making us all subservient weak-minded people by feeding us white bread, white rice, cereal that grows soggy in milk, and other dangerous foods. It was a fascinating piece of work. It became quite the conversation starter.

We announced the first opening with four days' warning. Mike and I were swamped selling licenses at all hours of the day and what little night there was. We answered the question of when the first opening would be innumerable times in person and on the CB and VHF radio. Once fishing started, we sampled fish and processed fish tickets until we started dreaming about them.

CHAPTER TWENTY-TWO

JAMES

One of the nice things during the king-chum rush was that Geiger allowed us to go to the cookhouse cafeteria that was set up for AC's employees. It actually got the job done better since we took our supper break with the folks on the processing line where we were sampling fish. We got more sampling done since we didn't have to prepare, cook, and clean up. We just took a supper break and returned to sampling.

Mike and I had sat down to our roast beef and potatoes when a familiar looking Yup'ik man stopped opposite us and asked, "May I join you?"

"Of course, have a seat." *Where do I know him from? We usually are ignored or avoided. Except for our friends.*

"Thank you, I haven't been back long enough to talk with the villagers. Guess I need to regain my accent. I'm James Mosses."

Mike was introducing us and asking where James had been. *Could be Mr. and Mrs. Mosses" son, but don't remember anyone mentioning another son. Don't really want to ask?*

James had shaken hands with Mike and was offering his hand to me. "Kim, you must be Irene's friend. Mom really speaks well of you. I was working for AT&T in Chicago when she died. Since Mom and Dad had just lost Tommy, I quit and came back to help them. They're taking it hard."

Irene died. Heard rumor of suicide. Don't ask how she died, none of my business. Doesn't sound like the family is angry with me. No secrets in the village, so they surely knew about Marie and I after Irene wouldn't speak to anyone after Tommy's accident. Was it an accident?

"Yes, Tommy JR.'s accident really hit them hard. I'm sure losing Irene made it doubly bad. Sounds like you're having a little trouble readapting to village life?" I said.

"Yeah, after being gone so long for high school and electronics school then AT&T. Really liked living in Chicago, but Mom and Dad really need me. I'm easing back in. Nice not having a supervisor, or time clock anymore," James said.

"Yeah, we don't have a time clock and Geiger is easy to work for," I added.

Our conversation shifted to current events in the village. I didn't even notice when Mike moved off to join a group of line workers our age. Then the shift got called back and Mike and I returned to sampling for age-length and sex of the commercial catch. Only ran into James a couple of times the rest of the summer. His dad must have been keeping him busy. I noticed they never did open their fish camp on the other side of the boat yard that year.

CHAPTER TWENTY-THREE

INTERAGENCY COOPERATION

"That's it, Bethel. Let you have the last word. KE6628 Emmonak, out.

"Emmonak, I do have some last words. An anthropologist from the University of Alaska is coming out, and we've agreed she and her assistant can have room and board there in the bunkhouse. They will be arriving today."

"Oh, boy. A babe," Mike said.

"Don't know what she looks like; anyway I'm engaged," I said, then keyed the mike, "Bethel, do you know what time? Emmonak."

"Bethel back, nope."

"Ask what she looks like?" Mike asked.

"Emmonak back, err have you met them?"

"Bethel back, nope."

"Emmonak back, well, the door is always open. Emmonak out."

"Bethel out with Emmonak. KE6628 Anvik River…"

"Great, now how do we know which plane to meet?" Mike asked.

"Since they didn't tell us which plane to meet, I presume they don't think they need to be met. We aren't hard to find, and I'm sure Geiger gave them directions. We just wait for them to show up. In the meantime, we need to eat breakfast and do the last fish tickets."

"Doesn't having a woman around excite you?" Mike asked.

"Nah, probably just going to be a pain in the ass. Marsha's the only girl I'm interested in. Anyway, you are surrounded by single girls. They aren't always working the slime line."

After breakfast, Mike decided we needed to sweep up. I went to work on the fish tickets and taking the verbal catch reports from the processors. Mike finished sweeping and we went to work on the dot sheet, which is easier with two.

One person calls out the fisher, the other finds the space opposite that fisher's name and under the date of the fishing period. If they already have a dot, you move on to the next, but if they don't have a dot, you add one. After all the tickets for the fishing period are checked, you count the dots under that fishing period. Then multiply the number of dots (fishermen) by the hours in the fishing period and you have the effort, fishermen-hours for that period. Then you can calculate the catch per unit effort (CPUE) which allows you to compare catch from year to year.

About lunch time, there was a knock on the door. Mike jumped up, only to collide with the anthropologist and her assistant, a male lower class man who had come in the open door. Mike showed them the available bunks and the little honey bucket room at the end of the row of bunkbeds. Depending on your sex or need, the small size of the room required backing in but, the door when opened, it blocked the view from the bunks. This provided a privacy "curtain" of sorts. Their backpacks on their bunks, they came out and we finished introductions and had lunch.

They were doing interviews, and Mike volunteered to show them around town that afternoon. I didn't complain, figured the dot sheet was done, the number of tickets was dwindling with the end of the king run and the chum run was past its peak. Anyway, Geiger had never actually made one of us crew leader, and we were supposed to help. Readon and Eric burst in on me about an hour after they left.

"Shit, forgot all about you guys. We've got a full house."

"What? You rented out our beds," Readon joked, but Eric looked a little concerned.

"No, we just have a couple of visiting anthropologists so you're going to get stuck with top bunks. Being a younger brother, I'm sure Eric is used to the top."

"Huh?" Eric said.

"Nobody lets him on top, not even his girlfriends," Readon jabbed.

"Hey, not true. You guys lay off," Eric ordered.

"Pick a bunk and let's get unloaded so we can get a shower and Muk'ai," Readon said, stepping into the bunk room.

Ready for a break, I actually beat them to the test fish boat resting on the boat yard's muddy beach. I filled my hands with gear and headed to the office. When I met Readon coming the other way, I said, "Salt."

He said, "Pepper."

Eric said, "What?"

Mike explained loud enough that I would hear, "It's some Iowa superstition his grandmother taught him."

Yep, amazing how much you learn about one another sitting around a few campfires.

The three of us made short work of the load. Leaving me with the nice ocean bright jack king they had caught on the last net check that morning, they headed for the shower house. I filleted the king and dropped it in the cooler for supper. Our supply of ice was down to ice water, but I just warmed some water on the stove and washed my hands. *Let someone else go for ice.*

Luckily, that had been the last fishing period in July. With six of us in the office, doing fish tickets would have been a pain. Instead, Readon and I were busy with a trip to Flat Island, towing the utility skiff to finish packing up the camp. Readon had put Eric to work on the annual recalking of the Wahoo so she wouldn't sink out from under them on their way upriver.

As we finished loading up the Flat Island camp Readon asked, "Did you see those guys displaying for that girl, like a bunch of dogs with a bitch in heat. Glad Nita's not far away. Wonder how long the survey will take in Kotlik?"

"Geiger thought it was too long last year, not sure the big village excuse will cut it now he knows about Nita. Even with Marsha in

Fairbanks, I'm glad I don't feel the need to impress the anthropologist like those other guys."

"Yeah, Marsha's a lot cuter."

"Nita has her beat too, considering you and I are such low hanging fruit. How did we manage such babes?" I said.

"Hey, speak for yourself. I'm grade A, all-Alaskan male."

My obscene comeback was drowned out by the test fish boat's outboard. I got busy starting the one on the utility skiff and followed him upriver.

CHAPTER TWENTY-FOUR

MARSHA ARRIVES

It only takes the subsistence crew, Readon and Eric, three or four days to re-caulk and paint the Wahoo. I seem to recall Readon finished Emmonak and moved surveying the rest of the Delta villages to Kotlik, not as centrally located as Emmo, but a lot closer to his heart. Poor Eric got stuck with being a third wheel. I'm sure the anthropologists weren't around much longer, but it felt like a month with that crowd in the bunkhouse. Marsha and I had plans for her two-week summer vacation to be spent in Emmo during the fishing closure, and we didn't want a crowd around. Mike had transferred to his next position and I was finally alone, waiting for the fall chum run and Marsha.

I met her plane at the Bethel runway and found my feet shuffling. The urge to run and hug that beautiful woman struggling with the desire to just soak in her walk from the plane. Running finally won out. Marsha always shows more decorum in public so she just watched me stampeding to her. I took her in my arms and bent down and kissed her. As my tongue worked its way into her mouth, she gently pushed me away and bent her head back.

"Not here, wait."

"Okay," I said disappointed. "Like I told you in the letters, it's been a good year. Everyone is happy, but almost everyone is out of town picking berries. It's kinda a summer vacation."

"I won't get to meet any of your friends?"

"Depends; I don't expect Geiger. I'll take you over to the Bering Trader for a tour of a cannery and introduce you around. Show you the

Coop and AC, not sure who all is staying to clean and repair during the closure. You'll get to meet the postmistress when we check for the mail before I take you to the office. I brought the boat for your gear. Usually we just walk, but thought I'll let you see Emmo from the water."

I saw the pilot add Marsha's suitcase and duffle bag to the luggage pile. The suitcase was a gift from her mother and the duffle bag a gift from me. The suitcase stuck out since it was the only one. As I collected the two bags, Marsha asked. "They don't even have a plywood ramp for the luggage? What if it's raining or snowing?"

"That's why I got you a waterproof surplus duffle bag; traveling in the bush means luggage often gets left out in weather."

"What's that guy doing?' she said, nodding to the old guy collecting the cargo and loading it into the small trailer behind his three-wheeler.

"He works for all the airlines I think; he meets the planes, delivers the mail to the post office first. He also includes as much airfreight as he can. I've never followed him, but assume he takes the freight to his house, then he delivers it to where it's going. We've only ever had one package, which he brought to the office, answered 'Doy' when I said 'Camai', not sure if he was busy or just doesn't speak English."

"Those Eskimo words?"

"No, they're Yup'ik. Doy means 'end, over, I'm done talking, now you can'. It's sort of the period at the end of a sentence, but more the end of a paragraph of speech. Handy, since you always know when it's your turn to talk. 'Camai' is another versatile word, it's both greeting and goodbye. Now you know about all the Yup'ik I do. You wait here till we get the mail." I stepped onto the first step I had kicked into the mud bank down towards the waiting boat. I used my heel to make it a little deeper for Marsha.

"Why don't you use Eskimo? I think you told me once that Eskimo is an insult."

I was loading the bags into the boat after improving all the stairs on my way down. I turned and started up, improving the stairs with my toes. "It isn't here, since no one knows except a few Yup'iks who are interested in Anthropology."

"I didn't ask about Anthropology. I wanted to know what's wrong with Eskimo?"

I reached the top. "Give me a chance to finish. When Kass'iks—"

"Who are…what's that word? Can't you just answer the question?"

"Kass'ik is us white people." *Don't mention special words for black people and Japanese. KISS, she doesn't like not to be talking.*

"The Algonquin tribe was the first one early settlers asked about the Inuits, who were their neighbors to the north. There wasn't a good fence, so they weren't good neighbors, and Eskimo meant enemy. Not really an insult but…"

"Kim, what are we doing now?"

What, forgot her rapid changes of mind. "Err, guess the boat is loaded, we need to get you in."

"That's not a problem." She scampered down the stairs to the boat.

Always forget, she's more athletic than me. I followed her down, more slowly and carefully. I picked the anchor up off the shore and rinsed the mud off in the river. "Do you think you can push us off and jump in when I get the motor started?"

"How?"

I put the anchor in the bow of the boat. "You just grab the gunwales like this," I said, grasping either side of the bow, "wait until I start the engine and push out, using your arms to lift yourself into the boat. Like I just did," I added as I clumsily lifted myself in over the bow.

"Hmm, guess I can do that. We always used the dock at grandpa's."

I stepped back towards the steering seat in the rear. I had to suddenly catch my balance as the boat moved out into the river's current. "Like that?" I heard from behind me. As I scrabbled over the center passenger seat, I looked back and saw Marsha grinning, pleased with herself.

"Not exactly, cutie. We usually wait until the pilot is seated and the engine is started. Now we're drifting uncontrolled down the river and we don't know if the engine will start."

While I spoke, I took my seat and lowered the outboard. *Should still be warm so skip choke.*

POP! The engine misfired on the first pull of the rope. I quickly pulled the choke out to the one-half setting and pulled again. The engine started chugging, belching a cloud of thick white smoke on the first two chugs. I pushed the choke in and the engine began running smoothly as I shifted it into forward. *Pretty smooth, could have been better.*

"Gee, granddad used to have to pull more times."

Okay, I'll take that. "Over there is the school and teacher housing. They are all gone for the summer."

"No summer school?"

"Nope, not that I've heard of. That white bunch of buildings is the new shower, laundry, and water treatment plant."

"Is that where the sauna is?"

"Yep."

"Do you think the women will try and burn me out like the guys did to you?"

"I don't think so. You girls are usually better behaved than us boys. Well, that's Honey Bucket slough next to the runway, where we started."

"Why do they call it Honey Bucket?"

"When the state built the airport, they dug the ditch to raise the runway. Since it comes out into the river, it has water flushing in and out with the tides and rain. So people started pouring their honey buckets into it instead of the river since it's a shorter walk. And it became Honey Bucket slough, even though it's really a ditch. Watch out, I'm going to speed up now."

I hit the throttle and speed upstream past the empty space up to the big floating processing barge where the Yukon Fisherman's Cooperative bought and processed salmon. Slowing down, I said, "This is the Coop, since you'll be here for the first Coho opening, I'll bring you down for a tour during operation. You'll get three tours that day, although AC and the Coop are pretty much the same thing. That's it; going upstream."

"That's all? Where do you stay?"

"Most of the town is downstream of the airport. Hang on, I'll show you." I hit the throttle and turned downstream. We raced down past the airport and I slowed down to just enough throttle to steer. "There's the school where we started. That Quonset hut is the movie theater most weekends. Gets really hot in there, so it's a good thing he only has one projector, so we all get a break between reels."

"What do you mean?"

"Didn't you know movie theaters have at least two projectors, one is showing the movie while they put the next reel on the second one, then get them in sync and start the next reel before the first ends? That way there's no break in the movie."

We were drifting downstream past a mostly vacant area. Some fish racks and smokehouses, a couple of old BIA (Bureau of Indian Affairs) houses, one vacant. Pointing, I told Marsha, "That one is still occupied, that other one is being disassembled as someone needs the lumber.

BIA tried to use a single design for the whole county and found out a house built for the Arizona desert cost more to heat in an Alaskan winter than two houses cost. So they redesigned the houses."

"You mean everyone gets a house from the government?"

"Yeah, pretty much. Not quite sure who gets chosen or how. Remind me to tell you more at the office. This is some old equipment that a contractor decided wasn't worth shipping out. This is the AC plant and freezer ship. The AC store is back there on the other side of the road. Our office is that sheet metal building behind everything. There it is, you can see it now looking back across the boat yard."

"What boats?"

"That open space next to the office is filled with tenders and other boats all winter. They're all out on the water working now. Hang on, sometimes I hit the beach a little hard." I ran the skiff gently aground and led Marsha into our new home.

The next two weeks whizzed by. Marsha adapted to life without running water smoothly, her only comment about the honey bucket was, "Grandmother's chamber pot was a lot prettier, but smaller. You need to use more Lysol when you flush."

Marsha was there for the first Fall Chum opening and proved to be an excellent data taker while I was sampling the catch for A-W-L information. While sampling, she got to watch the heading, gutting, and washing process that went on preparing the salmon for freezing. During breaks, she whispered and giggled with the women on the cleaning line. Her new friends she made at the shower and laundry. "Hey, what were you guys laughing at?"

"They were telling me about you hanging your shirts to dry with the arms out."

"Yes, my mom didn't teach me to just put the pins at the shoulders, so I pinned up the cuffs too. Guess I frightened a few people when I left them up all night."

"Yes, they were filling me in on all the things I was going to have to do for you."

"Great, you'll be a good Yup'ik wife and I can give up all this woman's work."

"Think again, bub. What was that last length?"

I measured the fish again. *No secrets in this place. Wonder what else they've told her.*

Marsha was a little shocked at the cannery, as most people are. "They leave the bones in?" she shouted over the running butchering line where the salmon were being cut into pieces and the pieces pushed into the cans.

"Yes, that's part of the reason there is so much calcium in canned salmon. The bones just dissolve in the pressure cooker."

She pretended to shudder, and we finished our quick tour. Putting the cannery inside the Bering Trader, a ship didn't leave much room for looky-loos. The manager did give her a box with a dozen cans of salmon.

The next day, I was hugging her so hard she begged, "Gotta breath!" "Sorry," I said, relaxing my arms. "You have Jonrowe's number in case your flight doesn't make it into Bethel."

"Yes, I'm a big girl and can handle the airlines and call for help if I need some."

We kissed and I watched her cute bottom in skintight jeans cross the glacial silt runway to the Islander that was making the milk run to Bethel that day. *Big girl? I guess she is 5'2" of dynamite. Glad she had a good time and made so many friends. We'll be alright if I ever get assigned to a village. God, I'm going to miss her. By the way, if You can spare a little time to keep an eye on her and the rest of the people on the flight, it would be nice.*

CHAPTER TWENTY-FIVE

FAIRBANKS

We were parted for only a couple of weeks instead of the expected four to six. The fish ticket editor for the upper Yukon had to return to college. Fred Anderson the Upper Yukon Area biologist had planned to replace him with the Middle Yukon catch monitor in Nulato (I think?). That catch monitor had an accident with the state's 50 CC motorcycle. His knee required surgery, so instead of transferring to work in Fairbanks he had to stay home to recover. These developments were good news for Marsha and I, since with the closure of the fall chum season in the lower river Geiger decided I was more valuable in Fairbanks than Emmonak. The duty station transfer happened faster than the mail, so I arrived at our basement apartment unexpected a couple of hours before Marsha got off work.

Probably should have had Fred drop me at Marsha's office. I don't have a key. Don't need a key! All the doors are open. The windows are too, and two big 48" fans are running, one in the bathroom and the other in the bedroom door. What happened? Everything got wet somehow and is being dried out.

I piled my gear in a corner of the bedroom that was dry. Investigating the scene, I decided the source of the water was the bathroom ceiling, which was new. Fairbanks was still in its warm, dry (little humidity) summer and the carpeted floor was dry. The fans were no longer necessary, but like gates, best to leave fans the way you find them.

I could walk to Marsha's office and surprise her there. Nah, here will be better. Oh boy, the three Rainer's I left are still here. If she had a boyfriend, at least he didn't drink my beer. Better stop that, she doesn't like being teased

145

about other men. Mmm, the beer tastes good. I settled into the bean bag chair with a book and my brew. *Almost as good as a loaf of bread, bottle of wine, and thou. Thou will be home soon, and who needs bread and wine if she's here?*

"Kim!"

Startled, I closed the book on my finger and nearly rolled out of the bean bag chair.

Regrouping, I put in my bookmark, dropping the book to the floor, struggling to get out of the bean bag saying, "Surprise, cutie!"

"When did—? Why didn't you—? Is the rug dry? It was horrible! They're raising the rent."

"Stop that, I need to talk!" The last was said as I tried to end her barrage of questions and statements with a kiss.

Putting my arms gently around her, I said, "Slow down and tell me everything." *Like this uniform. Marsha's not into role playing. Likes to take care of her clothes. Still would be fun to lay her in that outfit.*

"I opened the door and the smell was terrible. Don't know how they didn't notice. The pipe must have broken the day I left. There was shit and toilet paper everywhere. The carpet was soaked. It didn't make it into the bedroom, so the clothes were safe. I went upstairs and told her to get it cleaned up. She said, 'I have to wait for my husband to get home.' I packed my stuff and loaded Critter. He looked and wasn't happy when he got home. 'Why didn't you tell us sooner?' 'I told you I was going for two weeks.' 'We'll get it fixed and cleaned up, but the rent is increasing in October to six hundred dollars.' 'That's twice what we pay now!' 'I can get it with all these pipe liners in town so pay or move.' I wrote you. Why didn't you answer?"

"The letter must still be in the mail."

"Why don't they have a damn phone?"

"You know."

"Yeah, no phones. What are we going to do?"

Is it my turn to talk? I sure miss doy, at least you know when it's your turn to talk. "Where did you go?"

"Betsy took care of me. They're wonderful people. You're lucky to have them as friends. What are you going to do?"

"Hello, is the floor dry?" The owner arrived home from his job and gave me a break to think.

"I think so. At least I didn't find any damp spots," I said.

"I better check!" Marsha added and began moving about the apartment feeling the floor.

The owner and I were shaking hands. "Nice to see you back. Did she tell you about the rent?"

"Yes, guess we'll have to move. I only have a job for another month or so," I replied.

"Get right on looking for a place. They're hard to find, and you won't get anything this nice for less."

Yeah, how many people get to rent a septic tank? "Yeah, I hear you, Fairbanks is filling up."

"I can't find any wet spots; I guess you can take the fans out." Marsha arrived back.

"Good, the rent on these things is terrible. Everything is. In this town everything is going up," he said as he turned off and unplugged the fan sitting on the bathroom floor.

I walked over to the one by the bedroom door, doing the same as he began carrying his fan up the stairs.

"What are you doing?" Marsha whispered to me.

"Helping out," I said. *Sooner we get everyone out, the sooner I can take you to bed.*

"That's his job, not yours."

"Yeah, but I'm a helpful person," I said, coiling up the power cord and heading to the stairs. I met the owner coming back in the house.

He thanked me and took the fan out to his pick-up; with a little luck he would get them back before the rental place charged him for another day.

I went back downstairs and guided Marsha into the bedroom as she continued to ask and answer questions about where we would move to, how we were going to afford a new place and so on. I wasn't sure she knew she was being undressed until she pushed me away so she could hang her uniform up. Her questions and answers continued until I finally managed to get my tongue into her mouth and her pent-up passion like mine took control of our bodies.

CHAPTER TWENTY-SIX

SEPTEMBER 1974

The hills around Fairbanks were turning green and gold, the green the patches of spruce trees and the gold the fall leaf color of the alders and aspens. Marsha dropped me off at the office at Creamers Field, which was filled with migrating waterfowl. She then went on to a new dentist's office. She and her old boss's wife had a disagreement about the job duties of a dental assistant. She thought cleaning up after procedures included all the janitorial needs of the office. Marsha thought it meant sterilizing instruments and the work area between patients; vacuuming and scrubbing floors in the waiting room and offices were not the job of a dental assistant's duties in Marsha's view. She moved on easily to another practice.

I mostly edited fish tickets for the upper Yukon Fall chum fishery. Thankfully, I did get to drive down to Nenana or Manly to sample the commercial catch and pick up fish tickets. Edmund Lord, a catcher– processor– buyer in Nenana had been a problem prior to my arrival.

Chasing off the subsistence crew with a chainsaw. A restraining order had been needed for the staff to continue sampling. Marsha having a day off and riding along with me on my first trip seemed to solve the problem for me (see Alibi Mike).

Manly was a different situation. On my first trip, I discovered the commercial greenhouse. The owner gave me a tour of his jungle under glass. Tomato vines grew to the twelve-foot ceiling and then followed and twisted their way across the greenhouse. With warm water from the hot springs to heat and water them and the nearly twenty-four hours of sunlight, the tomato vines were rampant. The big red fruit was like nothing I had had since leaving Iowa. Rich, dark red tomatoes that exploded when you bit into them or cut them. I always managed to have some cash on those trips so I could buy tomatoes for Marsha and I.

The Commercial Fish Division was chartering a fish wheel out on the river where a crew was tagging fall chum salmon (see Alibi Mike). They sampled the fish they tagged and sampled the commercial catch. My trips were to pick up fish tickets from the buyer in the village and the A-W-L data the crew had collected. For reasons I've forgotten, I think it had something to do with the crew leader incompletely filling out Field Purchase Orders (FPO), I also had to settle–up the field crew's bills at the general store, which was run by a true Alaskan character. She was late middle-aged, even shorter than my 5'2" girlfriend, but her legs and arms that showed from her plaid wool shirts with the sleeves cut off at the elbow and her cutoff jeans were sinewy masses of muscle that threatened to pop out of her sunbaked skin.

At our first meeting, we were finishing up business. I had transferred the itemized list of purchases to the FPO, then turned it and pushed it across the painted plywood counter worn smooth by use. "Could you sign it please at the bottom where it says 'vendor'?" *Wonder if I could take her arm wrestling?*

"Sure." She bent to the task. "What's my title?" she asked, referring to the blank line below vendor.

"Oh, clerk, owner, whatever your position is here."

"Damn bean counters in Juneau, what do they know about life out here?" she said as she filled the line in with a flourish.

I took the FPO book to tear out her copy and read, "*Queen of Manly.*" Laughing, I tore off her copy, handing it to her. "Thank you."

"Do you think that will pass?" she said, grinning.

"Probably, this is only my second year, but I don't think they read this stuff, just look to see if the line is filled in."

She cackled, slapping her hand on the counter. "You got that right. Hey, I'm getting quite a few of these things." She pointed to five or six of the yellow FPO copies hanging from a nail in the wall behind the counter. "When will a check come?"

"I don't know. But I promise to investigate it when I get back to Fairbanks. Maybe you left your title off the others, Your Majesty," I said, bowing at the waist to her.

"Get out of here, you smart aleck, but don't forget my money, or it's off with your head."

We parted, laughing.

Back in Fairbanks, I dropped my briefcase on my desk and picked up the phone, calling the regional bookkeeper in Anchorage on the phone.

"Hi, Judy, it's Kim."

"Hi, what's wrong?"

"Gee, I suppose no one ever calls you except when something is wrong. I promise to call and just shoot the breeze next time."

Laughing, she said, "I doubt it, but what's up?"

"The Queen of Manly hasn't been paid for any of the FPO's she's gotten from the Tanana Fish Wheel crew, and wonders when Juneau is going to send a check."

"Who?" she asked, still chuckling.

"The Queen of Manly, at least that's what she puts on the title line of the FPOs. She owns and operates the general store there."

"Hmmm." I heard pages turning in the background with Judy's chuckle. "No, there is a problem. I don't see any FPO's from the fish wheel since Lance chartered it. There is no problem with the FPO's since you and Fred started completing them, but there have only been two recent ones. They haven't had time to clear through Juneau."

"Only two! The queen has five or six pink slips. I'll have to see if I can find what the trouble is on our end. I'll look into it."

"Is your fiancée happy to have you back?" Judy asked.

"Yes, it's great. We do need to set a date and call our parents. She wants to wait until no one will spend the money to come," I said.

"Why's that?"

"She doesn't think her mom can afford to come, so she doesn't want to leave her feeling like she should."

"Well, when my kids are old enough, they better not pull anything like that," Judy said angrily.

Mock anger, I think she's serious. Better talk to Marsha about this plan. "I'll tell her, but I'll leave you out of it. Bye."

"You do that! Bye."

I poked around in my desk for a while and found an 8x12 yellow envelope labeled FPO's in one of the drawers. It had FPO's for all the upriver projects. Not sure what happened in the personal turnover, but the envelope had been forgotten. Correcting the old ones, Juneau wanted the purchases on the receipt itemized on the FPO, which the crew hadn't been doing since it was already on the receipt. I edited the incomplete ones, added the latest, sealed them up, and put in an envelope addressed it to the Anchorage office, I added, 'Attention: Judy' and dropped it in the outgoing mail. Mystery solved, sort of, and fixed.

Marsha picked me up about five-thirty. She got off at five. I got off at four-thirty, and not having anything to do, joined the "staff meeting" in the Sportfish Division's shop. There was always beer and chips, but I was one of the last ones left by five-thirty, everyone else having gone home.

I climbed into the passenger side, "Hi cutie, you better drive, too many beers in the shop. Anyway, I'm tired of driving after my trip to Manly. Look at these tomatoes!"

"You and your tomatoes. They are good though, just like home." She was turning around in the parking area and headed towards the driveway. "They'll be nice with tonight's macaroni and cheese."

"Is that all we have?"

"No, we have a can of tuna we can put in it," she said, turning onto College Road.

"Hey, I was talking to some people, and they agree with the Sharps that we shouldn't wait till the last minute to tell our folks about the wedding. I really think we should call tonight before we go see Father McCafferty." We were attending his four-session premarital class; tonight was graduation. After some discussion, Marsha and I had settled on September 27th. She, because it had a seven in it, her lucky number, and me because moose season would be closed. There are priorities in life.

"I don't know. There are still three weeks. Mom might still decide to come."

"Cutie, your mom managed to raise six children on Social Security survivor benefits. I think she knows if she can't afford to come to the wedding. I doubt my parents will spend the money. Mom keeps the purse strings pretty tight."

"I want to wait. I don't want people wasting money coming."

"I'm going to call Mom and Dad. With this short notice they'll already be going to spend the next nine months waiting for the birth announcement. If they decide to spend the money, that's their choice. I should at least give them the chance."

"What birth announcement are you talking about? We haven't talked about children yet. I already took care of my brothers and sisters; I'm not ready for my own yet!"

"Cutie, a surprise wedding will make everyone back home think you're pregnant. They won't believe you aren't until next year." I walked over to the breakfast counter that we used for all our meals since we didn't have a table. I started dialing the big black phone.

"Who are you calling?"

"Mom and Dad, I told you."

"But I didn't say you could yet!"

"Already done." Direct dial was still relatively new in Alaska, and you got to listen to an interesting series of sounds as the call was transferred to a transmitter that bounced it off a satellite, then back down to earth. *I wonder how close the receiver is to Des Moines. Who do I know that would know?*

Marsha made a grab for the cradle, trying to hang the phone up. I was quicker and picked the phone up, holding it out of her reach. *Wonder if she'll think to unplug it from the wall? She's not very mechanical.*

"Hi, Mom, is Dad home?"

"Yes, but what's wrong?"

"Nothing's wrong, everything is great, but I have some news and thought he should hear too."

"Oh, I'll get him." Through the muffled phone I could hear her shout into the family room, "Dick, it's Kim, pick up the phone." His reply was barely audible through Mom's hand: "Why what's wrong?"

"Nothing, he just wants to talk to both of us."

Another click. "What is it, Son?"

"Probably not a big surprise, but Marsha and I have set the date. We are going to be married on the 27th."

"What month?" Mom asked.

"This month, September."

"Why so soon?" Mom blurted out.

"Oh we've been planning it for a while, but wanted to wait so you wouldn't feel like you had to spend the money to come."

"Why wouldn't we come? I can get out of school."

Marsha was jumping up and down whispering, "The phone bill, the phone bill, don't tell my mother."

"Well, this call is getting spendy, after the first three minutes it gets ridiculous."

"All right, but you better send a letter tonight with the details," Mom commanded; Dad added, "Bye, Son. Congratulations."

I put the phone back down and dropped the receiver into the cradle. "Okay, cutie, your turn."

"We can't afford all these calls. Mom can't afford to come. I won't call. Your parents won't tell Mom, will they?"

"I don't think so. Linda said in one of her letters it was better not to ask them to give news to Mary Jane. They aren't awfully close."

"Good, so they won't tell her."

Marsha started boiling water for the mac and cheese. I sat down on the floor with my back against the wall watching the news on the old black& white portable TV. I bought it for a penny at a dormitory auction. It went cheap since it didn't have a power cord. When I popped the back off, I found the power posts still had copper wire under the attachment nuts. Looked like someone had just ripped the cord off. Probably a story there, but I didn't know it. It was only a matter of a few minutes work to attach a new plug-in cable. Scrounging the cable from various trash bins took a lot longer. My friends and I had been watching it for the last two years. The penny had been well spent.

I was having a beer, watching the news, as Marsha lectured me about going against her wishes and calling. She also asked repeatedly if she should call her mother. The third or fourth time, instead of telling her she should, I said "Marsha, Tom is the oldest man in the family, I'll just call him and ask his permission to marry you. Problem solved." I got up to head for the phone.

"Sit down, dinner is ready," she said, crossing the floor with my plate of mac and cheese mixed with tuna. "It's none of my brother's business who I get married to."

"It's supper, not dinner, you city slicker," I said as I tucked in. We were still discussing who and when to tell our marriage plans to when we arrived at Father McCafferty's office.

He said, "Good, we can work on how to solve disagreements." Then asked each of us to explain our side. Marsha didn't get a fair hearing, Father just said, "Marsha, you really should call your mother. Oops, I was supposed to let you two solve this."

Marsha said, "I'll think about it."

On the way home, Marsha decided she should call her mother. But she made it clear it had nothing to do with what I had said and especially not what Father had said. "Priests have been pushing me around my whole life; they don't get to start again now."

We arrived home and she picked up the phone.

"What are you doing?" I asked.

"Calling my mother."

"No, you shouldn't," I said.

"What, I thought that's what you wanted."

"I do, but with the five hour difference it's two in the morning there. You better wait until morning."

The next morning, she called while I was in the shower.

CHAPTER TWENTY-SEVEN

BEFORE THE WEDDING

Fairbanks was having a perfect September. Jacket losing weather: chilly mornings that required a jacket, and warm afternoons that didn't; people always walking out of work without the jacket they wore in the morning. Moose season opened, revealing one of the cultural effects of the pipeline boom. Normally, many businesses were closed with only a "Gone Moose Hunting" sign on the door. This year, hardly anything closed; everyone was making too much money. Most people still fit in a moose hunt, but owners and employees worked out a schedule that allowed time off for moose hunting while keeping the business open. Really spoiled the hunt, since filling the moose box (usually Sear's largest chest freezer) took priority, and the usual camaraderie, drinking, and card playing suffered, at least among responsible hunters. Instead of returning to work relaxed and pleased, most hunters returned tired and grumpy. Hunting is hard work. Having time to enjoy reconnecting to nature and friends can be the difference between real success and just making meat.

Marsha and I were both working, our free time after work spent with our friends planning our wedding. We couldn't afford live musicians, but Jeff, a philosophy student who lived in Lathrop's basement, volunteered to record our chosen music on his reel-to-reel recorder. The plan was he would then DJ the ceremony and start each song in the correct place.

Marsha wanted real flowers on the cake, much to my dismay; unlike her, I like those hard sugar calorie bombs. She found a baker in town who liked the idea and did a great job. I also believe the twenty dollars for the cake was the most expensive part of the wedding.

Mom and Dad called with their travel plans. They would be arriving separately so Dad could spend a few days hunting with me before the wedding. Mom wanted to keep the days a substitute would be teaching her first graders to a minimum, so she planned to arrive on Thursday, the day before the wedding. Marsha's mother called and gave us her travel plans. To our surprise, she and Dad were arriving on the same flight. As we hung up, Marsha asked, "Do you think they planned it that way?"

"I doubt it, Dad likes you a lot better than your mom."

"Should we tell them?"

"No! If they did it on purpose, which I doubt, they'll think we think they don't like each other. Better to let them be surprised. Dad will really be cranked off if there's open seating and he has to sit next to Mary Jane the whole way."

We headed to the airport to meet the Pan Am flight that M.J. and Dad were arriving on. Looking around Critter, Marsha asked, "Where will everybody sit?"

"I've given that some thought. You, Dad, and the luggage will be in the back, and your mom will be up here next to me. Unless you want to squeeze in between your mom and me?"

"You think your dad will be alright with crawling into the back?"

"I hope so, the only other alternative would be you and me in the back, Dad driving, and your mom next to him. I don't think that will work since I'll have to give Dad directions, and you know how your mother talks nonstop, even if it's just reading billboards out loud. We'll never get there."

"Oh, she's not that bad," Marsha said, coming to her mother's defense.

"She used to read me the newspaper while I waited for you to come down. She can't stand silence."

I drove to the back of the airport parking lot where Critter would be safe from other car doors. "No, you need to park closer. Mom doesn't like to walk like us."

"Okay." I had already learned that even though it wasn't in the spoken vows the unspoken vows included, "I will, as long as I live let Marsha pick where we sit and park." I had also learned that unwritten vows are only to be discussed with other men. Marsha had not laughed at the draft marriage vows I had offered when we discussed writing our own, resulting in our choosing the traditional ones, with the deletion of obey.

We watched the sleek 707 pull up to the terminal from the big window in the boarding and disembarking area.

The weather was nice, so the ground-crew just pushed the stairway out to the plane. The passengers began disembarking down the stairs across the tarmac to a terminal door on the first floor. From there, they climbed a set of stairs to the departure lounge.

Dad was among the first passengers to deplane, casually dressed with no carry-on luggage. Marsha and I worked our way through the people waiting for deplaning passengers to greet Dad. Marsha turned back to the window after giving my father a hug. Dad and I shook hands; Francisco men didn't hug other men. People deplaning slowed, with increasingly larger spaces between singles and pairs. Then there appeared to be no more passengers.

Marsha turned to Dad saying, "Did Mom miss the plane?"

"She's on there. Believe me; nobody missed her." I could hear the criticism in his tone.

About then, the stewardess at the plane's door accepted a full plastic bag from someone inside the plane. M.J.'s full figure filled the passenger way as the stewardess stepped out onto the landing at the top of the stairs to make room. Mary Jane waved to the terminal, then turned to the stewardess as she juggled a purse, carry-on bag, and the plastic bag. I didn't think she had enough hands, but she did finally manage to start down the stairs with her arms around the plastic bag and a shoulder strap in each hand. Navigating the stairway looked very perilous; luckily, an observant member of the ground crew left what he was doing and went to the bottom of the stairs to steady her as she stepped off.

Dad grumbled under his breath to me, "She made me carry that damn bag onto the plane for her. I felt like a damned fool."

I should tell him to forget it. MJ is a little eccentric. Won't help, probably make things worse. Dad's pride is a pain. "Well, you didn't have to carry it off, and no one you knew saw you."

Dad grumbled something as I stepped up to help MJ and give her a brief hug (hugging women was allowed in my family, double standard all the way).

Mary Jane was talking a mile a minute, shooting questions at Marsha fast and not waiting for answers before the next one. Dad was in the lead, already following the signs to the luggage claim. I was next, both hands filled with a full plastic bag and a huge purse; Marsha was carrying MJ's actual carry-on that had come as part of her luggage set. She and her mother were bringing up the rear. Dad was so far ahead he couldn't be mistaken as part of our group. I was trying to keep everyone in sight, but finally lost Dad as he outdistanced us. Since we were all headed to the same place, I shortened my stride so the gals could catch up to me.

"Where's your father?" Mary Jane asked.

"He's up."

"Do I know your maid of honor?" MJ interrupted.

"She's a matron."

"Who's the best man?" fired my future mother-in-law.

"Dave," Marsha and I started simultaneously.

"Do I know him?"

"I don't..." Marsha started.

"Who's that?" Mary Jane nodded towards some stranger.

"Who?" Marsha said.

"He's on first, what is on second," I finished under my breath, wasted effort since MJ announced, "Luggage claim, the sign says," pointing to the sign directing us in the direction we were going.

This strange conversation continued until we reached the single loop conveyor belt that brought luggage from the secret depths of the terminal out to the waiting passengers. Dad was already at the end where the belt goes back into the wall; hardly anyone waited there. This was my favorite spot too. You didn't have to lift your luggage over the people stacked two and three deep at the beginning.

Wonder if I learned to pick up luggage there from Dad or my own experience?

At the outside edge of the crowd gathered where the luggage first emerged, I turned, facing Marsha and her mother. "You wait here with this stuff; Dad and I will get the bags," I said very quickly while dropping everything I was carrying at MJ's feet.

Seeing her purse on the floor, she stopped what she was saying and grabbed the strap, rescuing it. I disappeared to the far side of the luggage loop and stood next to Dad. As I watched, I could see a struggle of wills going on as Mary Jane tried to gather everything up and follow, and Marsha kept putting what she was handed back on the floor, trying to keep her mother at my designated meeting place. A guilty chuckle escaped as I nudged Dad and pointed out Marsha's struggle.

"Daughters and mothers always seem to fight," Dad said.

"Hmm, kind of like fathers and sons," I said, hoping I might head off any of our usual disagreements. *Just remember Kim, even when he's wrong, you don't need to correct him. Unless he's about to walk into a bear trap!*

The bags came around and we grabbed them and carried them to a spot close to the door. Leaving Dad with the bags, I went to Marsha's rescue. Only took a couple of steps and they arrived. Garbage bag being carried by a stranger, a common occurrence in Alaska airports in those days. You never knew when it might be you with too much to carry. Mary Jane was busy telling her version of Marsha and my story. With a disappointed expression, *think lust may have been his motive to help,* he escaped, Mary Jane still telling him about us. I don't recall if anyone had a chance to thank him.

I zipping up my jacket, I told the group, "Okay, everyone wait here. I'll bring Critter around."

"Who's Critter?" asked Mary Jane.

"That's the name—" Marsha didn't get to finish as Mary Jane said, "We all can go."

"Too long of a walk—"

"I can carry my suitcase and overnight bag," Mary Jane interrupted.

With all this luggage. I headed out the door. *Let Marsha and Dad deal with this.*

"You're not leaving me alone," Dad said from behind me.

I never asked whose idea it was, but Marsha and Mary Jane were waiting in the loading zone with all the luggage when Dad and I returned with the Land Cruiser. Dad and I jumped out and walked to the back. I told Marsha, "Get in front with your mom, Dad is going to sit in the back." Mary Jane continued as the two of them headed for the front of the car.

MJ hates dead air like a radio announcer. I unlocked the spare and swung it out of the way, opening the top tail gate then the bottom. "Hop in, Dad." Stepping out of his way, I noticed Marsha helping M.J. with her seatbelt. *How is this going to work? Guess she can get to the middle from my side.* Using the trailer hitch as a step and the edge of the door opening as a handle, Dad pulled himself in. As he turned to sit on the left side, he almost collided with Marsha, who was coming over the top of the driver's bucket seat. Dad caught Marsha's shoulders and helped her over.

"Oops, I didn't see you."

"I got you."

"Thanks for your help."

"You're welcome. Do you want the right or the left?"

In the background, M.J. carried on; not sure who she was talking to or about. Marsha and Dad were sorted out, Dad left and Marsha right. I loaded the luggage, I lifted the tailgate, lowered the top half of the top, then latched the spare tire into place. *That leaves me alone with Mary Jane in the front. Guess I'm doomed to a lifetime of being out foxed. Oh well, she's cute and not boring.*

As I buckled my seatbelt, Mary Jane said, "See, Marsha, there's plenty of room for you up here. Kim's going to be your husband. You should be next to him."

Yeah.

"Mom, there's more—"

I had started the car, which caused a brief interruption in the conversation.

"But there is plenty of room up here."

"I'm back here now, I don't want to—"

"Kim, where are we going?"

"To our friends the Sharps'."

"How did you meet them?"

"Steve, their oldest son—"

"How far is it?

"About ten—"

"Dick, when is Pat coming?"

"Thursday."

Hmm, one-word answers, that's the secret.

"Where are we staying?"

"Mom, I told you—"

"A stop light, I didn't think they had stop lights here. There's a Super Value. Do they have normal food?"

"Yes, Mom."

"Those look like barracks."

"They used to be." *But were converted to apartments.*

"Alaska Land," Mary Jane read. "Can we go?"

"Closed Memorial Day." *Don't go into the bankruptcy and general confusion going on with it right now.*

Mary Jane continued reading signs, and asking what things were, or who lived there. Usually, I didn't know who lived there, but she really didn't seem to want to know. We arrived at the Sharps' house on third; to my relief, Marsha climbed over the luggage, and I lowered her to the ground.

"I'll take Mom in. You bring the luggage."

"Yes, ma'am."

"Stop that. Your dad will think I hen peck you," Marsha said as she headed to the passenger door to help her mother. I could see Dad smiling in the glow of the streetlamp that had just turned on. As I unloaded luggage to clear a path for Dad. He asked, "I thought the sun stayed up all the time?"

"Fairbanks is south of the Arctic Circle, so the sun always sets even in June. Although, in June and July, it's so close to the horizon that we pretty much have twilight for the few hours the sun is set. Always have midnight baseball games on the Fourth," I explained as Dad stepped out.

"I see. Like at home, the days get longer and shorter just as they get longer and shorter here."

"That's right."

"Hi, I'm Bert Sharp. You must be Kim's Dad. You look alike," Bert said from the curb with his hand out.

People say that, but I don't see it. Must be true though.

Shaking Bert's hand, Dad said, "Dick. I want to thank you for taking such good care of Kim these last few years."

"Not a problem, Kim's the best trapping partner I've had. Always ready to go. Let's get this luggage in."

The rest of the evening was occupied with everyone getting settled in, followed by a couple of drinks to relax.

Marsha and I left about ten for the short drive to our basement apartment on sixth. "I'll be moose hunting for a couple days with Dad. What are you guys going to do?"

"Mom doesn't believe that Bev's dress fits me, so we're having a fitting tomorrow. Followed by I don't know. Oh, almost forgot," she handed me a fifty-dollar bill. "Mom's boyfriend gave her that for us to spend on the reception."

"Wow, that was nice of him. I can go wild at Gold Hill." "Be sure to save twenty bucks for the wedding cake." I gave her a hug and a kiss. "Looks like this wedding is going to happen." My hands began exploring her body and she pushed me away.

"Not tonight, I'm just too tired."

"Okay, I have to get up early tomorrow for the moose hunt."

CHAPTER TWENTY-EIGHT

❧

MOOSE HUNT

I woke up just minutes before the alarm, which I shut off. Looking at Marsha's beautiful face, lust flooded my brain. *Nope, you don't have time. Let the poor woman sleep for a change.*

I slipped out of bed and into the main room where I had piled my clothes the night before. Before getting dressed, I started the coffee percolator and a cup of water on the stove. I was in my long johns when the water came to a boil. I dumped a half cup of instant oatmeal into a bowl, adding boiling water and stirring until it was just thick enough. I poured a cup of coffee and had a standing breakfast at the counter. *Wonder if I'll get on permanent? If Rom can't get HQ to let him fill an FBIII slot with an FBI, I'm going to get laid off. Wonder how hard it will be to get in a master's program at University of Hawaii? Applying this late, may just have to head down there and start classes in the spring semester. That will be a nice honeymoon. Better than taking our parents to Mt. McKinley the day after. It's hell being poor.*

I dropped the spoon and bowl into the sink, filling them with water as instructed. *Marsha's making progress on civilizing me.* I finished getting dressed and my coffee, grabbed my rifle, and headed for Critter.

At the Sharp's, I knocked quietly on the door, not wanting to wake the sleeping household. Instead of Dad, Bert answered the door and ushered me into an active kitchen. Betsy was dishing out her sourdough blueberry flapjacks. Dad and Bert were already eating, so this next batch was mine.

Should I tell her I've already eaten? Nah, those pancakes are too good. There's always room for them. I sat down and dug in. *I'll walk it off moose hunting.* Bert was done, Dad waved off seconds. *Hmm, since he had three, is it fourths?* I accepted Dad's leftovers, saying, "Betsy this is enough."

"Are you sure? There's plenty of batter."

"No more, I'll need to walk today."

Dad and the Sharps continued talking, mainly answering Dad's questions about current events like the pipeline and such. I finished stuffing my face and we were off.

We got to Sportsman's Mall a few minutes before they opened. I was explaining my plans for after the marriage.

"I thought Fish and Game wanted to give you a permanent job?"

"Well, the regional supervisor does, but he has to clear it through Juneau, which isn't going to be easy since the job is supposed to be an FBIII position and I'm only qualified to be an FBI. My first summer, they wanted to hire me for a moose project, but I was two months short on my residency requirement so they couldn't hire me. This giving an FBI a FBIII job is a lot bigger deal. Hey, they're opening the door." I opened my door and stepped out. Dad did the same. Over the hood, I finished, "That's why the plan is for a Master's; that and my experience would put me on the FB III list."

"Why not stay in Alaska?" Dad asked. I was holding the door open to the brightly lit Sportsmen's Mall.

"Tried that. Ron and I even worked out a work study program. Dr. Morrow, who is dean of Fisheries, thinks I should get my masters at a different school than my BS. My advisor and Cooperative Extension tried to change his mind but he wouldn't. Which sounds like BS to me. Fuck him."

"Hey, you shouldn't use language like that. Don't let your mother hear any of that when she gets here."

Shit, guess I'm still their little boy. "I won't, Marsha doesn't like that word either."

"Good for her."

"Can I help you?" the clerk behind the hunting counter at the back of the Mall asked. Behind the counter was a glass faced gun cabinet displaying thirty or forty rifles and shotguns. The counter itself was glass, topped with glass sides. Inside were displayed just about every kind of handgun you could imagine.

Dad answered, "I need a moose license."

He reached under the counter saying, "I'll need your hunting license."

Dad answered before I could, a little angry and confused, "Yeah, that's what I said, I need a moose hunting license."

"Dad, it's just like Iowa you need a hunting license and a moose tag." Looking at the clerk, I said, "He needs a nonresident hunting license and moose tag."

"Okay, need the other license book," the clerk replied, swapping the 'book' pads of blank licenses about eight inches long and three wide. The top page was a white form that the clerk or customer filled out. Then came a piece of carbon paper that copied the original onto a yellow copy underneath, like the fish tickets I had worked with all summer. Except they had a pink copy that stayed in the book for the store's accounting system.

"Can I have your driver's license, sir?" the clerk asked Dad.

Grumbling, "I can write it faster than you can copy it," Dad fished out his wallet.

The clerk answered, "Sir, you're making three copies when you do these, and we've found most people don't press down hard enough."

It is like a fish ticket, a third copy for the vendor. The clerk was slowly, with a lot of pressure, printing Dad's personal info into the license book. "Have you ever tried to read your handwriting?" I said.

Dad's reply was a glare.

The clerk spun the license book around on the glass to face Dad and said, "Sign here, press down hard, you're making three copies. Be sure to put your license number on your tag. That will be two hundred and fifty dollars." [1]

"What?"

"Yes sir, the nonresident hunting is one hundred dollars and the moose tag is one-fifty."

"What can I hunt with just the hunting license?"

"Just small game, sir."

Good, those sir's will help keep him calm.

"Skip the moose tag then," Dad said as he started signing travelers' checks, grumbling, "Your mother always makes us get these damn things. I like cash."

I followed my angry father out the door. We climbed into Critter and headed out of town.

We headed up the Steese Highway, stopping at open areas and glassing with my binoculars for moose.

We crossed the flats, mine tailings that pioneer species like willows and fireweed were slowly revegetating. Moose love willows so it was decent moose habitat. I explained to Dad, "This is almost seventy years old, left over from the hydraulic mining days."

"What's hydraulic mining?"

"Instead of tunnels and open pits like they use in Iowa, big corporations bought up all the mining claims in an area. Each claim is forty acres, but usually it was just a couple of guys with a sluice box working a stream with shovels."

"What if they didn't want to sell?"

"That's what they make John Wayne movies about; you remember 'North to Alaska'. By hook or crook, they would buy up a valley, then there's a canal, hand dug—I'll show you a stretch of it soon. That came down out of the mountains, giving them the water pressure they needed to use huge hoses and nozzles to wash away the hills that used to be here."

"You mean this wasn't always flat!" Dad said.

"Nope, use to be low forested hills like you see in the distance and up ahead."

"Those aren't hills, those are mountains."

"Spoken like a true flat lander; the White Mountains, which are living up to their name since they're white now, are what you see behind the hills. By Alaskan standards, they are low mountains."

"This rock-covered flatland is all manmade. Why is so much of it still rock?" Dad asked.

"I didn't find out till I took Soils last year. The top soil is washed off first, so it's on the bottom. Then the gravel and rocks start coming down. Then, if they found a vein of gold they would start blasting between washings since the hose couldn't do much against bedrock. The rock with gold was then moved to a stamping mill. The rock started at one end and these steel water powered hammers would start making big ones into little ones, until it was fine sand, then it was washed in the sluice box, which separated the gold from the waste since gold is heavier."

"Yeah, I saw a gold panning demonstration once."

"The industrial process actually missed some gold, most of which has been recovered by panners since the big companies moved on. Recreational panners still work over the tailing and get some gold now and then. Not enough to pay for the bacon."

"I think that's a moose!"

I stopped and picked up the binoculars and looked where Dad was pointing, then handed them to Dad.

'Shit, it's just an old car with willows that look like a moose head. Thought for sure it was a moose. Why are there willows and stuff in some spots, but not everywhere?"

"Mostly because people come out and dig up tailings for driveways and such by hand, or if it's a construction company, with backhoes and bulldozers. Since the top soil came off first, it's on the bottom when people move the cobbles on top and expose the topsoil it revegetates. Soils Prof said if the BLM would just require miners to bulldoze the top of their mine tailings flat, nature would take care of the restoration. But they don't, so where the miners work you still end up with bare rock."

We got into the forested foothills after crossing the huge flatland area created by hydrolicminning. I pulled Critter over and stopped.

"Good idea. I'm ready to get rid of some coffee too," Dad said as I stopped.

"That's not the only reason. Follow me across the road when you're done." I stepped off the road and took a few steps off of the gravel right of way and onto the moss and spruce needles that covered the forest floor. Dad followed shortly and I said, "Look at this," pointing down.

"It's just…there are boards lining that creek!"

"That's because it's not a creek; this was hand-dug by miners working for the big hydraulic-outfits. Highway construction and erosion have filled most of it back in, but this stretch is still the way it got left when mining stopped. It goes miles up into the mountains, the elevation giving it the head pressure it needed to level those hills that used to be on that flat land we crossed."

"How old are those boards lining it?"

"Mining stopped like fifty years ago. I doubt they replaced the boards that year. This local spruce holds up well. I expect, if you dug into the algae covering it, they're probably pretty punky."

"Pop-Pop was a miner, you know."

"Yeah, but he worked in tunnels. These guys at least were outside and only had to worry about trees falling on them. Still a hard way to make wages."

Dad was halfway back to Critter so I followed.

We continued up the Steese, the spruce growing shorter and shorter. Alders and willows became more common in the low places. Then mossy clearings began replacing the forest, often with a small pool or pond of water in the center. There were still some ragged and short spruce, obviously struggling to live.

"Dad, we call this muskeg, looks like easy walking, but there are a lot of deep spots that swallow your leg. Once it freezes, it's good ptarmigan hunting, mainly in the spring. The males are still white and try to lead you away from the hen and her nest."

"You just ground-sluice them?" Dad said critically. [-]

"No, if I have the shotgun, I flush them. Unlike grouse, they flush pretty easily. Harder shot than pheasants since they usually flush down instead of up, so it takes a while to quit shooting over them."

"You don't always use a shotgun?"

"No, I'm my father's son, that's why that High Standard 22 pistol is there between us. If I'm walking for big game, I carry it to shoot grouse and ptarmigan for camp meat. Haven't caught up to you yet, but I'm sure I've shot more game with the pistol than any long gun I own.

"Hey, this spot is where Bert got his moose a few years ago. It crossed the highway in front of him. He stopped, grabbed his 270 (caliber of rifle), got out of the truck and shot it about seventy-five years out. The moose fell down, then got up and was staggering around toward the road.

Bert was trying for a second shot, but the moose's motions were so unpredictable he couldn't get a clear shot. When it reached the center of the road, it stopped and gave a huge sigh, dropping dead. Poor Bert, he said he's never dressed a moose so fast, worried that someone would come, needing to get past."

"Judging by the number of cars we've seen today, not much to be concerned about, except these D.O.T. rigs that have been heading for town," Dad commented.

"There's a big, three-season D.O.T. camp up ahead. Guess they send the equipment that can be used for snow removal south for the winter. They keep a caretaker there for the winter, but otherwise they don't keep this road open in the winter. That's where I borrowed a hose clamp that got Hildebrand's Maverick a few miles closer to Fairbanks. We're up in the Alpine Tundra zone now, not very good moose habitat."

"Yeah, I noticed. Not much to look at, like the Aleutians where I was in war. A woman behind every tree, but no trees."

It's beautiful, like a little forest all decked out in it fall colors. Guess plant morphology taught me to look a little closer. I won't point it out, don't need an argument. "That's the Steese Road house down in that valley and the D.O.T. camp just beyond. Good place to turn around. Thermos is empty. Do you want to stop for coffee or a beer?"

"A beer would hit the spot."

I figured.

Parking in front of the log structure, we stepped out of the bright daylight and into the gloom of the poorly lit roadhouse. The random assortment of chairs were upside down on the empty wooden wire spools that served as tables. We walked up to the bar/counter stretching across the room's back. There was a mirror behind the three-tier shelf of hard liquor. The back bar also had four or five different brands of beer displayed under the booze. On either side of the back bar, stretching to both walls was an assortment of fossils and minerals from the neighborhood gold mines. Mainly small placer claims operated in the summer by individuals, partners, or families. There was no one at the counter, Dad grew impatient and tugged on the bell pull hanging over the bar.

"Dad, you just timbered the bar! Good thing there's no one here."

"What the hell?" an impatient voice said out of the kitchen at one end of the bar.

Simultaneously, Dad said, "What the hell you talking about?'

"He's on second I think."

A beer belly preceded a gray-bearded man with a dirty white apron over a dirty white t-shirt and jeans out of the kitchen. "We're closed for the season," he announced.

"Could you still serve coffee or beer?" I asked. "Humph." He returned to the kitchen.

"Guess we might get what he's drinking," Dad said.

Our host returned, dropping a can of Olympia beer in font of each of us. "Four bucks and you drink it outside."

"FOUR BUCKS!" said Dad loudly.

"He just got here, doesn't know the prices," I said, laying out a five. "Keep the change," I said, picking the can up and turning for the door. Our host went back into the kitchen with the five. I stopped and turned. "Are you coming?"

Dad turned to me, saying loudly enough to be heard in the kitchen, "He rips you off, then you tip him?"

"Hey, that's the regular price here. He's closed and trying to get things shut down for the winter. We lucked out."

Dad looked at me, "Lucked out?" Then started following me.

"Hey, don't forget the most expensive beer you've ever had." *Hope our host is enjoying this.*

"I had this at Bert's last night, just water like Coors. For two bucks, it could at least be a Budweiser," he grumbled.

"We'll stop at the Four Corners on the way home so you can buy some Bud."

"Don't think I can afford it," Dad said as we went out the door.

"It's a liquor store on our way back, you might get a six pack for five or six dollars. Bud's too expensive for our budget. I mostly drink Rainier."

We drove slowly back, but no moose showed himself. Dad picked up a couple of six packs of Bud at the Four Corners, grumbling about the price all the way home.

CHAPTER TWENTY-NINE

MOOSE HUNT DAY TWO

We started earlier since Dad was licensed. It was still dark when we reached the Four Corners and turned onto the Chena Hot Springs road. At first, there were houses and cabins along the road, denser the closer to Fairbanks you were. It was beautiful as we reached a portion of the road where there was a mix of BLM lands and private inholdings. This is where we slowed down for the sunrise and to begin our watching for game. The boundaries between public land and private were not well marked. If we saw a moose along here there was a risk of taking it on private property without permission. Fortunately, we made it through that stretch without seeing a moose, just the wonderful fall colors whose intensity varied with the increasing intensity of the sun. We reached the boreal forest that was almost all BLM land. This forest of white and black spruce was broken up by patches of muskeg, creeks of various sizes, oxbows the Chena River had left behind, and occasionally the river itself. This mixed habitat with lots of edges was prime habitat for all kinds of wildlife.

The first game we saw was a pair of spruce grouse, known locally as spruce hens. I drove past them about ten yards and stopped. "Dad, you're the small game hunter; take the pistol, slip out the door and bag those buggers."

Taking the pistol out of its holster, he chambered a round. "Just roll down your window and backup, be just like pheasants back home."

"Err, okay." I pulled down my window and put Critter into reverse. *Hope no one is watching. His concealed weapons permit isn't valid in*

Alaska. Not sure if this is legal. I stopped opposite the hens. Dad stretched his arm across my chest. *Bang!* The empty cartridge case hit me in the face as it was ejected from the semiautomatic pistol. One of the hens dropped, the other stood looking at its buddy. Another bang and case in the face, and the second grouse fell.

"Geeze, that second one wasn't very bright."

"Spruce hens are not very wary. That's why I don't usually shoot them with a shotgun. Have to pick them up and throw them to get'em to fly. When you do get them to flush, they land on the nearest branch before you can shoot."

"It's more of a challenge to shoot them with the pistol," I said, dropping out the door and picking the two birds up. I took a couple of steps off the right-of-way, dropped one bird, and pinched the skin at the neck of the second while pulling down hard. The skin broke, pulling off the bird's breast, and ripping off at the tail.

Dad had joined me, saying, "I see you haven't forgotten how to clean birds. These are like quail; you don't need a knife." He was performing the same operation on the second bird. "Look at the crop. What is that?"

I looked at the crop of the bird he was holding. "Mostly blackberries, with a few salmon and blueberries thrown in. Looks like he seasoned it with a few spruce needles. Two weeks from now, and their crops will be busting with nothing but needles. One of the few critters who can eat them." I had taken the warm breast I had skinned into my left hand, hooking my thumb into opening in the center of the breast under the neck. Then I pulled the neck down and out with my right. With various snapping, tearing, and sucking sounds the bird came apart: The neck, wings, back with the peritoneum containing all the organs, the thighs, legs, and tail in a neat, bloodless package. "Give me that bird, no sense in both of us having bloody hands."

"You don't save the legs?" Dad asked.

I pulled the second bird, as Dad had taught me years ago, setting the breast down with the other on a plastic shopping bag brought to keep birds clean. Instead of throwing the other half into the woods, I showed it to Dad, grabbing one of the feet, pulling the foot up and extending the leg and thigh. "See, nothing there. I used to take'em off like we did with pheasants, but grouse are like ducks. There isn't enough meat to make a bite. Foxes have to leave something for the weasels." I tossed the carcass into the woods, put the two breasts in the bag and we returned to the car.

"Congratulations, Dad. You made meat in Alaska." I stuck out my bloody hand.

He didn't shake it. "I taught you that gag, know your audience. Damned expensive pair of birds."

"A friend advised me that you should never try to put a price on having fun."

"We need to introduce your mother to him."

"Yeah. Marsha was there. She's frugal like Mom. They had quite the talk. Think they agreed to disagree."

"I like Marsha, she's cute and smart, hard to imagine she'll turn into her mother, but they all do," Dad added.

"Marsha says she isn't going to let it happen to her, and her sister agrees with her. I haven't met Mary Kay yet; Michelle's too young to have an opinion," I let out some of our private talk.

"Can't imagine that little angel getting fat and motormouthed." [1]

Our conversation continued along similar lines until we reached a turnoff onto a four-wheel drive only trail. The homestead act had expired many years before, although this didn't seem to be public knowledge. Every year, it seemed like BLM discovered someone homesteading; sometimes they flew under the radar for ten or twenty years and made quite the stink when they were thrown out. The mining law of 1876 was still in effect. Most of the claims were legitimate, but some disguised homesteading. Forty acres could be claimed with your mining claim. I was explaining all of this to Dad as we bumped and crawled our way up the rugged trail.

"BLM has to allow access, which is why this trail exists."

"You think this guy is just homesteading?"

"No, you'll see it goes clear above the tree line, so I think it's a real claim. Only operates in the summer when there's running water to wash the gold out of the pay dirt," I answered.

"Are we trespassing?"

"Not until we get to the actual claim."

We continued our slow ascent, leaving the tree line behind until we reached a high ridge. "Lunchtime," I announced, stopping Critter.

"Here?"

"Yeah, we can glass a lot of area from here. Won't hurt to spend some time in case something decides to move. You can see the mine workings down in that valley where the road ends."

We ate sandwiches and finished our thermos of coffee, studying the 360-degree scene for game. After about half an hour the cold wind had driven us back into Critter for shelter. Dad promptly fell asleep. I got bored finally, looking for what wasn't there and started Critter up, making a Y turn to get headed down hill again. Dad slept through the turn, but the first pothole woke him up. By the time I reached the Hot Springs Road, it was too late to go all the way to the end. We continued road hunting towards Fairbanks.

"Moose," I whispered, "on your side."

"Huh, where?" Dad whispered back.

"About a hundred yards up on the right side of the slough."

"Oh, I was looking closer," Dad excused himself.

I stopped Critter. "We're out of sight now. I'll quietly sneak back and try for a shot."

"Is it a bull or a cow?"

"Couldn't tell, only saw its butt sticking out of the willows," I whispered as I quietly opened the door and uncased my rifle. I quietly chambered a round, walking back only to be startled by Dad as I turned behind Critter.

"Quiet now," I ordered, as I assumed command. We slipped off the road and onto the edge of the right-of-way, using the trees for cover. *Took charge and he didn't say anything. First time, I think. Guess I've sort of have been in charge last couple of days. Weird. Kim, pay attention, we're trying to make meat.* We reached the edge of the slough opposite of the moose. I stopped and studied it for a long time through the binoculars.

"Is it a bull?" Dad whispered.

"Can't see antlers or balls. I'm going to move closer for a better angle on the crotch. You wait here." Squatting down, I began a very uncomfortable sneak, stopping and glassing after every step. *If it is a bull, should I shoot it there? Bert said everyone shoots a moose in the water once, then never again. Freeze my own nuts if I dress him in the water.*

I was halfway across the slough crossing when Dad startled me, whispering, "Is it a bull?"

"I told you to wait. Don't know, can't see any sex."

"Just shoot it, it's close enough to the road we can get it in before anyone comes.

Geeze, the old poacher. Shooting cow moose is like child molesting among Alaskans. Then my career would be over. He doesn't realize how big they are. Not an Iowa whitetail two people can pick up and put in the trunk. Don't have a truck anyway. "No!" I hissed. *What should I do?*

"Shoot," Dad whispered back.

Whistling, that gets their attention without scaring them. I shouldered my rifle, locking my left arm in the sling to steady it. I aimed right where the moose's head and neck should appear when it turned to look for the whistle. I curled my tongue and pursed my lips, giving a short sharp whistle. The moose exploded out of the water and into the brush. I scrambled up onto the road, running towards the moose's direction hoping for a second chance.

"Damn," I gasped as I struggled to breathe.

"You should have shot the moose," Dad panted as he caught up with me. I waved him away like a fly.

"Let."—Gasp.— "Me."—Huff.— "Catch."—Inhale.— "My breath." I stood breathing deeply. *Never were much of a runner. Shouldn't run with a loaded rifle!* I pulled the bolt back, pushing the loose shell back down into the magazine, holding the shells down with one finger as I closed the bolt onto the empty chamber with my other hand.

Later, at Bert and Betsy's, over after dinner drinks, Dad asked Bert, "Don't you think he should have taken the shot?"

"No, he did the right thing, if you're not starving, shooting a cow moose is worse than murder. Part of the reason for that is that most murders that take place here are people who needed killing. Shooting a cow moose is leaving someone hungry next winter. [1] You should never shoot even a bull in the water. Made that mistake once, never again;

two of us almost drowned getting that moose out. Lastly, and most importantly, he was thinking ahead about his career. He and Marsha won't starve if they don't get a moose, but if he shot a cow, he'd never work for the Department again.

CHAPTER THIRTY

❦

THE WEDDING

Marrying Marsha was the most important thing that happened in my life. Sadly, my memories of the day are a jumbled mess. This chapter will cover the highlights.

I dropped Marsha off at the Sharp's with her dress and assorted wedding paraphernalia. We each had a list of things to do that day.

First on my list was baking the unleavened bread for communion at the service. I had found several recipes and ended up with three loaves for tasting. Unleavened bread is easier than yeast breads since there is no waiting for it to rise or kneading the dough. The results are rather heavy and dependent on ingredients for flavor. Like fruitcake, but not as sweet. The chosen recipe was supposed to go into the wedding scrapbook, but has gone missing. My recollection is that it was a whole wheat soda bread. Better than the standard stick to the roof of your mouth communion wafer, but not by much. Baking and clean up done, the reception was in our apartment; I had clear orders; I didn't get to pull a 'leave cleanup for Marsha' trick.

There's a gap in my memory here, probably because I was cleaning house, which is rarely memorable. We had originally announced the reception as being BYOB, but Mary Jane had given me the fifty dollars that her boyfriend had sent for beverages. He worked for the Iowa Alcoholic Beverages Division and wanted us to party hard.

I arrived at Gold Hill, my regular liquor store. Normally I would be buying whatever beer was on special. I was surprised to be greeted at the door with, "Congratulations, Kim. Hey everyone, Kim's here. Today's his wedding."

People seemed to come from everywhere to shake my hand and congratulate me. Gold Hill was attached to a large house, said to have been the mine manager's back in the day. I never did figure out who all lived there, marital status, or any other details.

I do recall a shaggy, skinny guy who was stocking shelves, who was new to me, asking, "Who are you?" as he shook my hand. The owner, built like a pro-wrestler with a full beard, slapped me on the back, saying, "This is Kim Francisco, one of our best customers. He's getting married today. What can we get for you?"

"My mother-in-law's boyfriend gave us fifty bucks for booze, I thought champagne."

"What kind and how much?"

"Err, I know zilch about champagne, I'm at your mercy." I was following him through the shelves to the champagne racks.

"Hmm, weddings often have a magnum." He picked up a huge bottle. "Then use a bunch of these little champagne glasses and everyone gets a taste for the first toast." He had motioned to a stack of little plastic champagne glasses in boxes.

I don't know. Marsha doesn't drink much. It's BYOB, if people want more they always have what they brought. But the wedding I was at where they did that, I don't think there was enough, barely wet my whistle.

"Your friends are pretty big drinkers. You might want to get a case of the standard bottles. I'll buy back what you don't drink. That would probably be the cheapest way to go."

"Yeah, Marsha likes frugal. I'll get a case."

"White or pink?"

They were talking about what they needed, borrowed, blue, no blue champagne. I usually drink red but rose is okay.

"Let's try pink. Hope it doesn't clash with anything."

Chuckling, he said, "I'll meet you at the cash register. Have to get the case out of the back."

I met him at the register, then loaded the case into Critter. *Remember John, Dad's salesman? He was bringing back the champagne and realized he was just an ornament in his wedding. Drove off, stopping at first small town bar he hit. Carried in the champagne and he and his new friends drank it all up. Wonder how the owner felt about all the free drinks?*

Dad took everyone out to supper, at least, I think that was before the wedding. Marsha looked gorgeous. She was wearing a gown her best friend had given her in high school, after a prom or something. It was rose, made from a soft velvet fabric. Marsha normally wore very little make-up. She didn't need it; Mom, Mary Jane, and Betsy had helped her go all out. Her make-up was still subtle, but brought out her gorgeous brown eyes and pink lips, surrounded by her long beautiful light brown hair with blonde highlights. She called it dishwater blonde, but I had never seen any dishwater that color.

Things really get hazy now. Jeff, our sound man, missed his cue and Nights in White Stain didn't start until Marsha was halfway down the aisle. I flash onto following Father McCafferty around as we served communion. I remember the kiss after being pronounced man and wife; I didn't want it to end, and Marsha had to gently push me away.

I remember signing all the paperwork afterwards and wondering what business does the State of Alaska have with my marriage. Marsha had slipped the house key to one of the women in the dorm and they decorated our apartment before we got home. The rest is pretty much a drunken blur, except I remember how cool Bert Sharp looked standing with a drink in one hand, his pipe in the other, with one leg up on something.

Since we were taking Mom, Dad, and Mary Jane to McKinley Park (Mountain and park are now properly named Denali), Marsha insisted we clean up before going to bed. I seem to remember a few folks stayed behind to help with the cleanup.

Finally, in bed, I asked, "Do you want to consummate our marriage?" "I'm too tired. We took care of that this morning."

"Yeah, we did." I kissed her goodnight. Marsha went right to sleep. Ron had called the last day I worked. My hire as a permanent biologist had gone through.

I do remember my last thought as I went to sleep. I thought, *Wife, job, and career; guess I just graduated to adult.*

OTHER BOOKS BY KIM FRANCISCO

ALIBI MIKE and His Gang of Parasites on the State The Experiences of a Fisheries Biologist's First Summer in Alaska Pristine Press and Media

FLYING FISHERIES BIOLOGIST

Flying experiences of an Alaskan Fisheries Biologist in Pristine Press and Media

ABOUT THE AUTHOR

This is the author's third book, the second in his series of biographical memoirs, which begins with ALIBI MIKE. Kim is now 72 years old. Don't let them kid you; there is nothing young about it. As you read in the dedication my wife of fifty years passed away while this book was struggling to be published. Born and raised in Des Moines, Iowa, he became an avid angler, hunter, and trapper. He finished his education at the University of Alaska Fairbanks. While attending university, he began working for the Alaska Department of Fish and Game, Commercial Fisheries Division for twenty-two years. Fish and Game field employees were much more likely to be killed on the job than state troopers and had a 20-year retirement plan as part of their benefits package. After two years as vagabonds, Kim and Marsha settled in Lucas, Iowa. Kim was asked to apply for a vacancy on the Iowa Natural Resource Commission and recently completed twenty- one years on the commission. The longest-serving commissioner currently. He resides on seventy-eight acres of restored native prairie, wetlands, and forest. The property is in a perpetual conservation easement, Marsha didn't want all the hard work to be ruined by a new owner.

Connect with Kim Francisco: https://kimfrancisco.online/

Metamorphosis